The Solzhenitsyn– Sakharov Dialogue

Recent titles in Contributions in Political Science
Series Editor: Bernard K. Johnpoll

The First Amendment Under Siege: The Politics of Broadcast Regulation
Richard E. Labunski

Political Culture, Foreign Policy, and Conflict: The Palestine
Area Conflict System
Basheer Meibar

The Politics of Wilderness Preservation
Craig Willard Allin

Nationalism: Essays in Honor of Louis L. Snyder
Michael Palumbo and William O. Shanahan, editors

Compromised Compliance: Implementation of the 1965 Voting Rights Act
Howard Ball, Dale Krane, and Thomas Lauth

City of the Right: Urban Applications of American Conservative Thought
Gerald L. Houseman

The Conservation of Enemies: A Study in Enmity
Frederick H. Hartmann

The American Governorship
Coleman B. Ransone, Jr.

Strategic Studies: A Critical Assessment
Colin S. Gray

Keeping a Finger on the Public Pulse: Private Polling and Presidential
Elections
Bruce E. Altschuler

The Quest for Nuclear Stability: John F. Kennedy and the Soviet Union
Bernard J. Firestone

The Solzhenitsyn– Sakharov Dialogue

Politics, Society, and the Future

Donald R. Kelley

Contributions in Political Science, Number 74

GREENWOOD PRESS
Westport, Connecticut • London, England

Library of Congress Cataloging in Publication Data

Kelley, Donald R., 1943–
    The Solzhenitsyn-Sakharov dialogue.

    (Contributions in political science, ISSN 0147-1066 ;
no. 74)
    Bibliography: p.
    Includes index.
    1. Soviet Union—Politics and government.
2. Solzhenitsyn, Aleksandr Isaevich, 1918–   —Political science.   3. Sakharov, Andreï Dmitrievich, 1921–
—Political science.   I. Title.   II. Series.
JN6511.K38   947.085'092'2   81-13258
ISBN 0-313-22940-6 (lib. bdg.)   AACR2

Library of Congress Catalog Card Number: 81-13258
ISBN: 0-313-22940-6
ISSN: 0147-1066

First published in 1982

Greenwood Press
A division of Congressional Information Service, Inc.
88 Post Road West, Westport, Connecticut 06881

Printed in the United States of America

10   9   8   7   6   5   4   3   2   1

Copyright Acknowledgments

The author and publisher are grateful for permission to reprint from the following works.

Andrei D. Sakharov, *Alarm and Hope* (New York: Vintage, 1978). Reprinted by permission of Random House, Inc.

Andrei D. Sakharov, "How I Came to Dissent," *New York Review of Books*, 21 March 1974. Reprinted with permission from *The New York Review of Books*. Copyright © 1974 by Nyrev, Inc.

Andrei D. Sakharov, "In Answer to Solzhenitsyn," *New York Review of Books*, 13 June 1974. Reprinted with permission from *The New York Review of Books*. Copyright © 1974 by Nyrev, Inc.

Andrei D. Sakharov, *Progress, Coexistence, and Intellectual Freedom* (New York: Norton, 1968). Reprinted by permission of W. W. Norton & Company, Inc., and Andre Deutsch Limited.

Andrei D. Sakharov, "Tomorrow: The View from Red Square," *Saturday Review: World*, 24 August 1974. Copyright © 1974 by *Saturday Review*. All rights reserved. Reprinted with permission.

Specified excerpts (passim) from *The First Circle* by Aleksandr I. Solzhenitsyn, translated by Thomas P. Whitney. Copyright © 1968 by Harper & Row, Publishers, Inc. English translation copyright © 1968 by Harper & Row, Publishers, Inc. Reprinted by permission of Harper & Row Publishers, Inc.

Alexander I. Solzhenitsyn, *From Under the Rubble*, translated under the direction of Michael Scammell (Boston: Little, Brown, 1975). Copyright © 1974 by YMCA-Press, Paris. Translation copyright © by Little, Brown and Company, (Inc.). Reprinted by permission of Little, Brown and Company and William Collins Sons & Co. Ltd.

Specified excerpts (passim) from *Letter to the Soviet Leaders* by Aleksandr I. Solzhenitsyn, translated by Hilary Sternberg. Copyright © 1974 by Aleksandr I. Solzhenitsyn. English translation copyright © 1974 by Writers and Scholars International Ltd. Reprinted by permission of Harper & Row, Publishers, Inc.

Specified excerpts (passim) from *The Oak and the Calf* by Aleksandr I. Solzhenitsyn, translated by Harry Willetts. Copyright © 1975 by Aleksandr I. Solzhenitsyn. English translation copyright © 1979, 1980 by Harper & Row, Publishers, Inc. Reprinted by permission of Harper & Row, Publishers, Inc.

Contents

Preface

To write about Alexander I. Solzhenitsyn and Andrei D. Sakharov as dissidents is hardly a new endeavor. Both have been the subject of countless essays detailing the nature of their activities and the considerable personal price that has been exacted from each. Yet, perhaps understandably, emphasis in that literature has fallen principally on their courageous opposition to an increasingly repressive regime, and on those aspects of their writings that are critical of the present Soviet order; less attention has been given to their programmatic views of the kind of society that ought to be created to replace an ossified bureaucratic state struggling to maintain control over an increasingly dynamic and restive society. What is generally known in the West is often a gross caricature of a complex reality. Solzhenitsyn is pictured, at least since his forceful entry into the debate on Western attitudes toward the Soviet Union, as a reincarnated Slavophile anxious to condemn the seductive perversions of Western society and to assert the inherent superiority of the "true" Russian national character, while Sakharov is viewed as the embodiment of Western democratic values and as a proponent of the emergence of Western-style democratic institutions in the USSR. To be sure, there is at least partial truth in these characterizations; Solzhenitsyn is enamored of the importance of the unique experience of his nation and sees it as the key to the future, and Sakharov is, with qualifications, a proponent of the creation of an open and democratic system in the Soviet Union. Yet to accept such simplistic images as wholly definitive of the political philosophies of Solzhenitsyn and Sakharov is to distort reality, forcing it into the comfortable, if misleading, frame of reference commonly applied in the West. This particular reality is, as usual, more complex than our first comprehension, and it is the purpose of this study to deal with that complexity, recognizing that the political philosophies of these two important dissident figures are a product of their unique life experiences, their assessment of the present order, and their hopes for the future.

This study also makes the argument that, in one very important sense, the Solzhenitsyn-Sakharov dialogue has important analogues in other advanced industrial nations attempting to resolve the crisis of identity of modern society. No less than other nations that have achieved the status of mature industrial powers, the Soviet Union now finds itself pondering the relationship of the past and the future, both officially, through modifications of Marxist-Leninist doctrine and the creation of the "new" dialectical stage of "developed socialism," and unofficially, through the dialogue described at length within this study. It is not surprising, then, that many of the issues and concerns raised in the West about the nature of modern society and its interface with its cultural traditions should find their reflection in the writings of Solzhenitsyn and Sakharov. Nor should the reader be amazed that the dissidents and oppressors alike address themselves to the same problems, at least in terms of the substantive concerns about the evolution of Soviet society.

Any discussion of the political philosophies per se of Alexander Solzhenitsyn and Andrei Sakharov must cope with several difficulties in terms of sources. In Solzhenitsyn's case, any comprehension of an expressly political philosophy must be gained both from his explicit polemical works, more frequent in recent years, and from his literary oeuvres and autobiographical works, which weave together complex themes of personal experience, political commentary, historical analysis, and moral philosophy. His denial of overt political aims is less an impediment than is his continued isolation, even in exile. Andrei Sakharov's writings, while fewer in number, are more expressly political in nature and confront more directly the questions of the nature of a desirable alternative future. Yet in recent years, especially since Solzhenitsyn's exile in 1974, Sakharov has increasingly focused his attention on the day-to-day concerns of the dissident movement rather than on any further explication of his earlier programmatic works. This is certainly understandable, given both the increasing pressure brought to bear on the dwindling dissident community and Sakharov's own growing disillusion with the prospects for reforms. It does, however, confront any student of his political views with a shrinking universe of commentary from which to glean Sakharov's innermost reactions to the wholly negative changes around him, a phenomenon now made even worse by the writer's internal exile to Gorky.

For the sake of the reader, and in an attempt to provide easy access to the most complete commentary by both authors, English-language sources have been cited in the references, although quotations offered in the text have been checked against the original Russian versions, when possible. The nature of the original sources and the translations are discussed at length in a bibliographical essay at the end of the study.

Special thanks must also be given to a number of institutions that aided me in various stages of this study. The American Philosophical Society provided an initial research grant in 1978 to examine as yet unpublished *samizdat* materials, access to which was provided by the Center for International Studies at the Massachusetts Institute of Technology and the Russian Research Center at Harvard University. A considerable portion of the final research and writing was accomplished while I was a fellow of the National Humanities Institute of the University of Chicago, an endeavor funded by the National Endowment for the Humanities, and additional support was subsequently made available by Mississippi State University, where I was then teaching. My personal debt to other scholars who have pondered the meaning of dissent in the USSR and the writings of Solzhenitsyn and Sakharov is too extensive to review in detail in this preface, but it is acknowledged, when appropriate, within the text itself.

The Solzhenitsyn–Sakharov Dialogue

1

The Origins
of Dissent
in the Soviet Union

The reasons why dissent arises in any modern society are always complex, in part the product of its political traditions, and in part a result of an interconnecting web of circumstances, personalities, ethnic and national loyalties, real and imagined grievances, political strategies, and social philosophies. Dissent within the Soviet Union certainly mixes all of these elements and more, reflecting both the ethnic and philosophical diversity of dissident groups, and the post-Stalin regimes' oscillations between flirtation with reformers, critics, and even dissidents, and their periodic but never completely successful attempts to repress critical elements. But to note this complexity is not to explain why the dissident movement came into being in the mid 1960s, why it grew to encompass a broadening spectrum of the society, and why, by the early 1970s, it had grown to such a stature in the eyes of the world that public opinion compelled Soviet leaders to deal cautiously with leading figures such as Alexander Solzhenitsyn and Andrei Sakharov even as less well known dissidents were subjected to harsher penalities.

To pose the question of why dissent arose at all in the Soviet Union is, at least for some Western commentators, to beg an obvious question. Why, indeed, should it not arise, given the revolutionary heritage of pre-1917 Russia, the murderous and only partially officially lamented excesses of the Stalin era, and the continuing closed nature of the system which denies any meaningful political role to all but a small elite? Yet to point to these factors alone is hardly to explain the relatively recent phenomenon of dissent. Repression was even more severe during the Stalin era, when millions of real or imagined critics were swept into the camps during both the purges of the thirties and the postwar years. And it is no more satisfying to suggest that the relatively light hand applied during the Khrushchev era was the true cause of the upwelling of critical commentary that emerged. While it was certainly a contributing factor—the "thaws" of the period and the occasional factional exploitation of dissent-related themes certainly broke the silence of the previous era—the short-lived remission of tight controls did little to provide the real substantive themes which have filled the pages of both officially sanctioned and *samizdat* publications.

Adding to the complexity of explaining dissent in the USSR is the obvious fact that many facets of Soviet life have changed for the better since Stalin's death. While the common person enjoys no meaningful political rights as they are understood in Western democratic society, he now lives better in material terms, so much so that one commentator has dubbed the Soviet state under Brezhnev "welfare-state authoritarianism."[1] And as Jerry Hough has repeatedly pointed out in his numerous writings, the level of citizen involvement and participation in governmental and quasi-administrative tasks has grown dramatically in recent years; while far from conveying real political power to the new citizen-participant, these changes do bring him into personal contact with the machinery of government and permit him to enjoy some impact on the implementation of policy, particularly at the local level. Even more importantly, such controlled participation is seen, at least by Soviet leaders, as hopefully providing an even closer sense of citizen identification with the regime.[2] Professional and occupational groups have also enjoyed a greater degree of professional autonomy and increasing influence, especially within their areas of technical expertise. Numerous studies of Soviet decision making since the death of Stalin have traced the emergence of groups such as economists, planners, writers, lawyers, the military, educators, and many more and noted their gains (as well as their losses) in terms of influencing policy decisions once reserved exclusively for top-level Soviet leaders.[3] Valerie Bunce and John Echols III have gone so far as to describe the USSR under Brezhnev as a "corporatist" state—a mutually beneficial arrangement in which the major interests and power blocs are represented and their views taken into account in policymaking, and in which the party provides a centralized coordinating, planning, and legitimizing role.[4] In such a setting, coherent direction is provided by the party, which consults widely among an admittedly closed circle of quasi-autonomous groups and elites regarded as crucial to the maintenance of the system. In return, these elements accept both the necessity of coordination and the party's monopoly over the selection of key personnel (exercised through the *nomenklatura* system), and its right to select and define legitimate political issues as the necessary quid pro quo of their enhanced role. What is significant about the notion of corporatism is that it presumes the existence of a political formula which has tacitly governed the exercise—and the restraint—of political power during the Brezhnev years, a formula that provides for the articulation and mutual adjustment of a selected range of opinions and defines a set of unwritten rules of political battle. It implicitly suggests the existence of a reasonably well tuned political mechanism that has proven itself at least grudgingly responsive to pressures from certain quarters to loosen controls over some policy areas and to co-opt, however defensively, elements of the society whose skills are regarded as crucial or whose passive disaffection or open resentment are to be avoided.

Yet, despite these efforts—admittedly highly selective in terms of the elite and professional groups co-opted—and despite growing attention to the proconsumer and welfare-state dimensions of public policy, dissent continues. Indeed, from the mid 1960s until the onset of more severe repressive measures in 1972, it grew, spreading both in terms of mobilizing new elements of the society and generating increasingly sophisticated critiques of the Soviet system, and in terms of acquiring an international audience, first through the activities of notable dissidents such as Solzhenitsyn and Sakharov and then, more systematically, through a conscious effort to draw upon support abroad and to form organizational ties with groups such as Amnesty International.

The reasons for the emergence of dissent in the Soviet Union are a complex amalgam of political and social factors which marked the first two decades after Stalin's death. Facilitated in part by the vacillating nature of Khrushchev's rule and in part by the broadening of the range of public discussion and politically active elements within the party and the society, the tone of post-Stalin Soviet politics became less still and muted than during the *Vozhd's* brooding dominance. With the initial competition among Stalin's lieutenants came a cautious diversity of policies and appeals to various potentially important audiences—Beria's short-lived appeal to non-Russian nationalities; Malenkov's "New Course," which initiated the first "thaw" in Soviet literature and held forth the prospect of greater attention to consumer demands at home and "peaceful coexistence" abroad; and Khrushchev's own initial conservative appeals to the forces that opposed the "New Course," which eventually gave way to his own version of economic and political reforms that broke with the Stalinist past. What had changed was both the style and the content of Soviet intraelite politics. As competing leaders turned to other elements of the elite for support, both new issues and old grievances were brought forward, some of which were highly critical of Soviet society in general and the conduct of Soviet politics in particular.

It must be remembered that the major events that loosened, however temporarily and incompletely, the bonds on literature and social commentary and emboldened the regime's critics were seen by those who initiated them primarily as tactical weapons to be used against their enemies within top leadership circles, or as attempts to stake out and legitimate new issues, new policies, and, hopefully, new supporters in the battle over Stalin's succession or the struggle to define the limits of collective leadership. Simply put, they were a part of the new style of Soviet politics, and to raise the issues of political reform, of greater freedom of expression in the arts and literature, of the treatment of non-Russian peoples, and, ultimately, of the excesses of the Stalin era itself, were quintessentially *political choices*. It matters little whether one views Khrushchev as an inconsistent "harebrained" schemer or as a well-meaning but clumsy reformer, to accept the argument that the events which gave impetus to the public emergence of dissent— his 1956 denunciation of Stalin and the "cult of the personality," his repeated returns to the de-Stalinization issue, and his occasional encouragement of critics of the Stalinist past such as Yevtushenko and Solzhenitsyn—were essentially political maneuvers against his foes. To be sure, they also bore a tangible relationship to the reformist bent of Khrushchev's policies at the time; at the very least it can be argued that Khrushchev's hopes for the rapid evolution of Soviet society toward communism required a decisive break with the past, one initiated as much for its symbolic import as for its immediate practical consequences. But the particular form that break took—a denunciation of Stalin's oppressive rule, with no clearly defined understanding of where the new limits would be drawn, and eventually the involvement of potentially dissident elements in the denunciation itself—unintendedly set the stage for the emergence of a self-sustaining and increasingly critical dissident movement.

Even if they suspected the nature of the Pandora's box they were opening—and it is clear that Khrushchev's conservative critics anticipated the worst—Soviet leaders of the late 1950s and early 1960s could not have foreseen another significant political development within the emerging dissident community: Soviet dissidents themselves quickly became highly skilled protagonists, learning to exploit the growing *samizdat* network; to form both formal and informal links among dissident groups seeking diverse goals; to use the legal system to greatest advantage, sometimes with modest success; to draw upon the visibility of leading dissidents; and, most importantly, to draw upon public opinion in other nations, expressed both through a diverse assortment of concerned and usually highly vocal audiences among writers, artists, scientists, and political activists in the West, and through an assortment of international human rights groups. While no one could describe the record as one marked by success after success, especially after the tightening of controls in 1972, it nonetheless remains true that Soviet authorities have been compelled to move with caution, tacitly adjusting the severity of their repressive measures when international protests are most strident, or blunting their attacks against some key dissidents such as Solzhenitsyn and Sakharov. This is not to suggest, of course, that a clear cause and effect relationship exists; Soviet authorities have at times resisted the efforts of their domestic and international critics and have surrendered much-desired goals such as trade opportunities with the United States for the sake of maintaining the position that the treatment of dissidents is a purely internal matter. Yet, in other instances they have proven more tractable, suggesting that vocal criticism from abroad may be judged too high a price to pay for the suppression of a particular critic, and perhaps that Kremlin leaders may themselves be divided on the severity of repressive measures.

If tactical political considerations on the part of the competing Soviet leaders provided at least an important part of the motivation to open the door slightly to some of the regime's critics, deeply rooted and as yet poorly understood changes in the nature of Soviet society itself provided the more profound wellsprings from which the major philosophical indictments and reform programs eventually came forth. This in no way diminishes the significance and liberating impact of events such as the denunciation of Stalin or the disclosures of the scope of Gulag-related activities; later critics for whom the nature of the camp system or the issue of greater artistic and creative freedom were not the principal causes of their dissent still admit that the disclosures of 1956 and the repeated return to de-Stalinization were important, both in raising their own level of consciousness and in emboldening themselves and other members of the intelligentsia to offer public commentary. But as the real *substance* of the dissidents' critique of Soviet society emerged, it became apparent that these discordant voices spoke not only about the need for freedom to discuss their views and grievances openly, but also about the major changes that had been wrought in their society by forty years of Soviet rule, and about the course of its future development. In some ways, they resurrected a long-standing debate about the nature, pace, and tolerable costs of social change that most recently had been heard in the late 1920s between critics and supporters of the New Economic Policy (NEP). While the specifics of the debate had changed—the level of industrialization and modernization had been irrevocably advanced and the structure of society fundamentally altered by the three decades gone by—the basic concerns remained the same: was the nature of contemporary society acceptable, and what should be the course of its future development?

Both the intensity of the critique that came forth and the multiple and frequently conflicting strains of the discussion that emerged are attributable to the fact that Soviet society in the late 1950s and early 1960s had reached two critically important social and economic phases in its development. On the one hand, the pace of social change that marked the Stalin era had appreciably slowed, and a stable social structure had emerged. While hardly a bourgeois society by Western standards, Soviet society came, at least in the eyes of its critics, to evince many of its worst features and excesses. On the other hand, in terms of economic change, a new phase of development was quietly entered in the 1960s. As the Soviet Union matured as a modern industrial economy, it became increasingly dependent both upon advances in science and technology for its further advancement into what Western commentators have termed the "second industrial revolution," and upon the development of more sophisticated planning and managerial skills to operate an increasingly complex society.

The creation of a reasonably stable middle-class society was a development earnestly welcomed by many within the Soviet Union. Indeed, it had much to recommend it: gone were the initial traumas of industrialization and collectivization; and now seemingly also absent were the fears and uncertainties engendered by the purges and the occasional campaigns for vigilance. As Vera Dunham has perceptively observed in *In Stalin's Time*, the regime had tacitly struck what she terms "the big deal" with the emerging middle class.[5] In exchange for their loyalty, their acceptance of essentially conservative standards of personal and social conduct, their reasonable efforts to advance the economy, and, above all, their political quiescence, the regime would provide a tolerable degree of both real and psychological security, of material comforts, and of hope for personal advancement.

But, on the negative side, the "deal" also did much to create what its emerging critics saw as a closed, rigidly stratified, smugly self-satisfied, and highly intolerant social order. The worst excesses of a petty bourgeois mentality appeared in the careerism and crass materialism of the new Soviet middle class, as did a sort of innate, don't-make-waves conservatism. The sense of dramatic and selfless purpose, and the *elan vital* of earlier years when individual commitment and sacrifice were seemingly linked to the betterment of society and the advancement of the cause, gave way to boredom, to a growing malaise, and then to the knowing but feckless cynicism described in Alexander Zinoviev's *Yawning Heights*.[6] To be sure, not all who saw the transformation judged it so harshly, and most simply accepted the welcome calm and the better life without a second thought. But those few who did react against what they saw began looking for something to fill the void, some hoping to find it in a return to "true" socialism, some seeking it in an extension of democratic rights to the society as a whole, some looking for it in a resuscitation of traditional national or ethnic values and cultures, and some searching for it in a reliance upon science and technology to move a static society forward once again and animate a new excitement about progress and a better future.

Walter Conner has perceptively pointed out that the social differentiation of Soviet society by the 1960s was also an important factor in the emergence of dissent.[7] Itself the product of three decades of industrialization and modernization, this differentiation produced not only the new Soviet middle class, but also a complex array of professional and occupational strata and groups, each with a growing awareness of its own special place within the social order. In most ways, these new strata were a part of the new middle class itself and clearly the beneficiaries of "the big deal." Yet in other ways there was an inherent tension in their situation: as they came increasingly to perceive themselves as identifiable groups with distinct interests and with, as they saw it, the right to play a role in policy formation, they ventured near the boundaries established by the "deal," which mandated that they play the game according to rules set down by the party. Most were content to accept the party's willingness to broaden their role gradually as it, too, recognized their importance in maintaining the system, and from this process slowly emerged the sort of "corporatism" described earlier. Others, however, hoped for more rapid or more fundamental reforms, some clinging to the hope that a quasi-pluralist society might emerge as a consequence of further modernization and differentiation. And as those hopes were dimmed by the restrictive aspects of the "corporatist" arrangement, some turned from moderate reformism to active dissent.

The second transformation which began in the 1960s was more a growing crisis in confidence about the continued relevance of the techniques of social and economic guidance, and about the adaptability of the economy and society in responding to the need for sustained growth and modernization. While some critics of the middle-class society produced by the success of Stalin's "big deal" stressed the negative social and cultural features of a petty bourgeois mentality, others focused on the need for extensive reforms of the ossified planning and administrative hierarchies, and for a revitalization of industry and science. To be sure, some reforms were attempted almost immediately after Stalin's death. Malenkov's "New Course" held forth the prospects for an extensive, if politically flawed, series of reforms in the economy, and Khrushchev's entire tenure in office was marked by repeated attempts to reform the party and state hierarchies and to revitalize the economy. While less frenetic than his predecessor, Brezhnev has continued, and in many ways intensified and deepened, reform efforts to make use of the "scientific and technological revolution" in the economy and in management, although important concessions have been won by conservative forces in both party and state who oppose the pace of reform.

The realization that a serious problem existed intensified in the late 1960s both as economic growth and productivity rates sagged for the economy as a whole, and as it became increasingly apparent that the reforms attempted to date had either been conceptually flawed, or their implementation blunted by conservative opposition. For many who had hoped that moderate reforms in the economy and of the heavy-handed bureaucracy would gradually result in a relaxation of political controls and the recognition of at least limited pluralism—for a brief period, Dubček's "socialism with a human face" became their model—the late 1960s produced a rude awakening. Instead of a process of evolutionary reform, they witnessed the repression of the Czechoslovak experiment, an intensification of efforts to suppress dissent within the Soviet Union, and the half-hearted and timid application (and frequently the outright failure) of the very reform efforts that were to be the impetus of more significant political change. The indictments that arose from these once-hopeful critics now condemned the current regime, at the least for its inept and cowardly application of reforms, and at worst for its unwillingness to adapt its style of leadership to the needs of a mature industrial economy. With increasing force, the charge became that the Soviet leadership was incapable of managing a sophisticated economic and social order and unable to initiate the sorts of policies and reforms that would restore the forward momentum of development. Whether because they were simply incapable of mastering new scientific and managerial skills, or because they were unwilling to pay the political price involved, Soviet leaders increasingly came to be seen as one of the major factors retarding the further evolution of society, be it toward some higher form of socialism, as some preferred, or toward a pluralistic democratic order, as others hoped.

THE GROWTH OF THE DISSIDENT MOVEMENT

Despite their common origins in the rejection of the Stalinist past, the dissident elements that emerged in the 1960s grew from diverse and varied roots and eventually brought forth a complex, and at times contentious, assortment of groups and points of view. Surveying the field of dissidents, Andrei Amalrik claims to discern three major philosophical schools of thought—"true Marxism-Leninism," "Christian ideology," and "liberal ideology"—while other critics of the regime such as K. Volnyi and Roy Medvedev group the various strains of the opposition movement according to their "liberal" or "radical" views, or their status as "neo-Stalinist," "conservative," or "Party-democratic" elements.[8] Western commentators have generated even more complex schemata of the dissident movement which highlight not only political philosophy, but also other factors such as nationality, ethnic identity, form of organization, political tactics, and so forth.[9]

This diversity was not readily apparent as the dissident movement gradually emerged after the death of Stalin in 1953. To be sure, limited dissent had occurred even before his death. For a brief period immediately after the war, Soviet leadership seemed unwilling or perhaps merely unable to squelch the inevitable postwar grumbling of the population or the claims of some elements for better treatment. Unanimity seemed absent within the top elite itself, permitting critics such as Ye. P. Varga, who challenged the

Kremlin's assumptions about the West, to voice their views openly for a brief period of time. But for the most part, such critics fell victim to the forceful reassertion of Stalinist orthodoxy after 1948. The only remaining open dissent came from a small number of non-Russian nationalities who had been forcefully removed from their native lands for real or imagined collaboration with the enemy; from resistance force in the once-independent Baltic states now incorporated into the Soviet Union; or from guerrilla bands in traditionally resistant areas such as the Ukraine who refused to lay down their arms after the war.

Stalin's death was both a political and psychological turning point. Long before Khrushchev's open denunciation of Stalin, a process of quiet de-Stalinization was begun, marked both by the limited release of political prisoners from the Gulag camps, and by the tacit acceptance that some sort of reform was inevitable. Beria's attempts to mobilize the support of non-Russian peoples resentful of decades of Russian dominance and an official policy of Russification briefly raised hopes that the suppression or re-location of certain nationalities would be ended, but his quick fall—motivated only in part by opposition to his position on non-Russian nationalities—ended speculation that a more tolerant policy was at hand. Malenkov's "New Course" marked a fundamental and more far-reaching departure from the Stalinist past. While it did not court the support of real or potentially dissident elements, it did palpably loosen controls over literature and the arts and permit some of the more liberal of the established writers to explore heretofore forbidden themes such as the insensitivity or malfeasance of high officials (always with the clear implication that the shortcomings were attributable to the individual and not to the system), or the stifling impact of two generations of cautious conformity and toadying to the whims of higher authorities. But with Malenkov's fall in 1955 at the hands of a "conservative" Khrushchev, who had successfully played upon opposition to the economic and foreign policy implications of the "New Course" rather than its less immediately evident consequences in terms of loosening controls over intellectual life, the drive to revitalize Soviet literature as a medium of social criticism temporarily lost momentum, in part because of the more conservative tone of Soviet politics in general, and in part because the more radical critics of the regime had not yet ventured into public view.

New impetus to the regime's critics was quick in coming. Khrushchev's denunciation of Stalin at the Twentieth Party Congress in February, 1956, went even further than Malenkov's "New Course" in challenging the basic tenets of the Stalin era and seemingly opening the door even wider to the possibility of further reforms. While the motivations for the direct attack on his predecessor were linked more to the vagaries of Kremlin politics of the moment—a newly "liberal" First Secretary now found himself facing opposition to his proposals for economic reform, foreign policy, and a revitalization of the party—Khrushchev also unquestionably understood the importance of a symbolic break with the past. The decision to denounce the worst excesses of Stalin's rule provided such a double-edged sword. In symbolic terms, while the exact details of the indictments contained in the so-called secret speech were not intended for general public consumption, it was planned that through a carefully controlled series of briefings of party activists and agitators, the general tone of the comments would be communicated to a mass audience. And in political terms, the carefully tailored charges levied against Stalin, and the examples chosen as illustrations of the consequences of the "cult of the personality" provided the cutting edge for Khrushchev's attack against his conservative opponents, who were tacitly linked through a thinly concealed guilt by association, or because they were the obvious beneficiaries of Stalin's actions. Without doubt, the nature of the threat was apparent to those at whom it had been aimed, and they were quick to take advantage of unrest in Poland and Hungary seemingly inspired by Khrushchev's speech. By the winter of 1956–1957, the First Secretary had suffered several important setbacks in terms of asserting the party's role in the economy and his ability to maintain his protégés in positions of power. But by the spring, he had once again regained the initiative, this time by shifting focus to a proposal for economic reforms rather than de-Stalinization per se. While the threat of continued de-Stalinization obviously played a critical role in motivating the attempted coup against Khrushchev in June, 1957, its possible implications in terms of opening the door for dissent were virtually ignored.

In fact, potential critics of the regime were slow to respond to the opportunities offered by the denunciation of Stalin, possibly in part because they well remembered the short-lived "thaw" of Malenkov's "New Course" and were reluctant to expose their innermost thoughts, or in part simply because the unpredictable oscillations between orthodox and conservative positions left them bewildered concerning the intentions of top leaders. Paradoxically, perhaps the most vocal of the regime's critics were the intensely nationalistic Georgians, who bitterly resented the decanonization of their former patron. On the more positive side, the denunciation gave new life to a muted debate within literary circles on the limits of acceptable criticism, with the spotlight falling on the deliberations of the editorial board of *Novy Mir,* which vascillated between orthodoxy and cautious dissent from 1956 to 1960.[10] The publication abroad of Boris Pasternak's *Doctor Zhivago,* and the regime's harsh response when its author was awarded the Nobel Prize for literature, created a brief flurry of protest and undoubtedly left a bitter residue of distrust within literary circles.[11] Most significant in the long run, however, was the accelerated release and sometimes selective rehabilitation of Gulag inmates, who returned to lead what the regime hoped would be quiet lives on the periphery of Soviet society. Only a few truly dissident journals briefly appeared in this period, and with the exception of the Crimean Tatars and the Meskhetians, who organized to protest that their traditional homelands had not been restored to them as a consequence of de-Stalinization, no effective protest groups came into being.

The last four years of Khrushchev's rule marked significant changes in the dissident movement; not only did major dissident figures emerge as individuals (admittedly sometimes to be exploited as weapons in intraparty battles), but also the movement acquired a dynamic of its own which sustained it independently of the vagaries of elite politics. Most visible were Khrushchev's repeated attempts to return to the question of de-Stalinization and his use of dissident themes to inculpate his conservative opponents. At the Twenty-First Extraordinary Party Congress in 1959, the First Secretary once again proposed further de-Stalinization, only to find his efforts blunted by the collaboration of remaining Stalinist elements and other less conservative figures who simply resisted the further concentration of powers into his hands. The battle was again joined at the Twenty-Second Congress in 1961, and this time Khrushchev scored greater gains. Stalin's body was removed from the mausoleum on Red Square, and the event was publicly commemorated by the publication of Yevtushenko's poem, "Stalin's Heirs"—an epithet obviously intended to brand the First Secretary's opponents, who, according to the poem, longed for the dictator's return.[12] Khrushchev pressed his victory over the next few years and, in a critical decision in 1962, once again turned to a literary medium to carry the attack by sanctioning, despite obvious opposition in the Presidium, the publication of Solzhenitsyn's *One Day in the Life of Ivan Denisovich*.[13]

The publication of *One Day* also once again linked the political fortunes of Khrushchev with the literary strain of the reform movement. Yet, even without significant encouragement from above, the debate within literary circles had intensified in the early 1960s. *Novy Mir* was again the focal point, and the battle was joined not only within its editorial board, now dominated by liberal reformers, but also by other more conservative journals. Even with the officially inspired quiet withdrawl of *One Day* from circulation as it became apparent, even before Khrushchev was removed from power, that the discussion it sparked had far-reaching and perhaps dangerous consequences, dissident elements continued to speak out. Several *samizdat* journals were founded by dissident groups, most notable among them being the brief-lived *Phoenix*, which first linked literary and political themes. In addition, individual dissidents began direct appeals to top Soviet leaders. Andrei Sakharov wrote directly to Khrushchev concerning the dangers of nuclear testing, and the dissident military officer Pyotr Grigorenko addressed a similar appeal concerning the party's deviation from a true Leninist course. While the authorities began to strike back by incarcerating their more vocal critics in mental asylums, as yet there was no widespread campaign to suppress dissent or stifle the few *samizdat* publications that had come into existence. But, from 1960 to 1964 it still was not possible to speak of a dissident movement per se; the few groups that were founded had little impact in fostering greater awareness among a wider audience of potential dissidents, and no effective links were established between them.[14]

The last four years of Khrushchev's rule also marked a perceptible increase in the number and intensity of protests linked to religious and ethnic dissent. Dissident priests within the Russian Orthodox Church grew increasingly critical, not only of the regime's malevolence, but also of the timidity of church leadership. Various splinter sects also openly criticized government repression. The Baptists, who had always been a target for government harassment, openly spoke out in defense of their rights. The Tatars and the Meskhetians also intensified their efforts to return to their homelands, with the latter forming an effective network of groups among its own people long before other dissident elements began to organize in any real fashion.

The coup in October, 1964, which removed Khrushchev from office, while a magnificent study of the vagaries of Kremlin politics, had little to do with the question of dissent. While there is good evidence to suggest that the First Secretary's critics felt a sense of unease about the Pandora's box he had opened, the specific issues and indictments raised in the Politburo and subsequent Central Committee sessions that presided over his demise dealt with his initiatives for economic reform, his management of party affairs (especially his attempts to force older cadres to modernize their approach to economic and social leadership), and, above all, his frenetic personal style of "harebrained" leadership. To be sure, the old guard still feared him, but it was now more because he was promoting younger, more talented cadres to positions just below those of the "generation of 1939" that had risen as a consequence of the purges and urging the old guard itself to learn new methods of leadership, rather than because of any overt return to the de-Stalinization campaign.

The new Brezhnev-Kosygin leadership, which emerged with an obvious mandate to restore stability and morale within the party, initially followed much the same line of silent repression that had been laid down by their predecessor. While the word was quickly passed to senior party cadres that de-Stalinization was a thing of the past and that the new regime would show a healthy "respect for cadres"—meaning that senior figures could once again feel secure in their positions and expect to have a reasonable say in party affairs—it was not until the Sinyavskii-Daniel trial in 1966 that a palpably more repressive position was adopted, and it was not until 1968 that the party officially laid the de-Stalinization issue to rest by proclaiming that the consequences of the "cult of the personality" had been extirpated.

In the two year period between Khrushchev's fall and the tightening of controls in 1966, the dissident community continued to grow, albeit at a slow pace, and to become more outspoken, both through the traditional medium of conventional literature, and through the formation of expressly political journals such as *Politicheskii Dnevnik* ("Political diary") and *Sfinks* ("Sphinx"). The former cataloged the regime's offenses against human rights and offered a forum for mostly liberal and democratically oriented views, and the latter took on a vaguely Slavophile tone. Small groups of dissidents were also now more numerous, the most significant of which was SMOG, which was more concerned with promoting free and candid discussion than with advocating a particular point of view.[15]

The arrest of Andrei Sinyavskii and Yuri Daniel in the autumn of 1965 cast the first shadow across what had been the new regime's cautious approach to its critics. While both writers were known to be active in dissident circles and, perhaps more importantly, had permitted their critical works to be published outside the USSR, neither author had launched upon any new initiatives against the regime at the time of his arrest, nor was either a publicly visible focal point of the opposition outside of the small dissident community itself. But their arrest and the months of uncertainty over the disposition of the case became catalysts for new protests, which grew in scope and intensity until the trial the following spring.[16]

While the obviously rigged trial of Sinyavskii and Daniel quickly arrived at the denouement intended by the authorities in handing down near-maximum prison sentences, its political impact produced results exactly opposite those that had been desired. For the dissident and the near-dissident alike, the trial became a major *cause celebre*, and its proceedings became widely known both through the expanding dissident grapevine, and the *samizdat* publication of a transcript reconstructed from the notes of those few dissidents who had been permitted to attend. The trial was also the first event to focus world attention on the phenomenon of dissent in the Soviet Union. While both authors' works had been published abroad, they had attracted little attention from a wide audience until their arrest. Still more stirring in the eyes of Soviet and Western observers alike was Sinyavskii and Daniel's decision to plead innocent and contest the validity of the law under which they were prosecuted, making the transcript which circulated widely both in dissident circles in the USSR and in the West a public counterindictment of the regime itself.[17]

Contrary to the regime's intentions, the conviction of Sinyavskii and Daniel and the sense of outrage it produced actually led to an increase in the level of dissent over the next two years, until the Soviet invasion of Czechoslovakia. Even though the antidissident drive itself intensified over the same period—late in 1966, Article 190, permitting incarceration for "slander injurious to the Soviet state," was added to the criminal code to provide a more tenable legal footing for future trials, which were quick in coming and increasingly frequent over the next few years—the dissidents always seemed to be one step ahead of those who would silence them. Even the most telling blows, such as the arrest or incarceration in mental institutions of major figures including Vladimir Bukovskii, Alexander Ginsburg, and Yuri Galanskov, or the open attack on Solzhenitsyn within the Writers' Union at a point when he was still hopeful of bargaining for the publication of *Cancer Ward* in the USSR, did nothing to slow the growth of the movement and the emergence of new groups and *samizdat* publications such as the *Chronicle of Current Events*.[18]

The political tone and texture of the Brezhnev regime at that time did much to lend support to the notion that, even in light of attempts to tighten the screws, there were forces at work that would eventually lead to significant reforms. The Sinyavskii-Daniel affair was read more as a moral victory than as a legal defeat, and the use of mental institutions as prisons was interpreted as a desperation move made by nervous and uncertain leaders. Just as significantly, the regime itself had begun to initiate limited economic and managerial reforms that, if successful, would modernize and rationalize the ossified and conservative bureaucracy which had resisted (or merely enveloped) even Khrushchev's forceful attacks. In the mid 1960s, it was not difficult to believe that the regime itself had set forces at work that would substantially modernize the economy and society, and thus inevitably (or so the theory went) result in greater social and political pluralism. And if this were the case, the reformers' best strategy lay in encouraging the "liberal" factions within the leadership, whose interests at least partially coincided with those of the dissidents. The fall of the Stalinist Novotny regime in Czechoslovakia late in 1967 and the initiation of liberal and far-reaching reforms during the "Prague spring" led many dissidents who hoped for gradual evolution toward pluralism and perhaps even an outright democratic order to think that "socialism with a human face" might be possible in the Soviet Union as well. The growing momentum of the liberalization in Prague through the summer of 1968 was watched by dissidents with increasing fascination and by Soviet leaders with mounting fears that, as in Poland in 1956, events there would spark similar liberal movements in other satellite nations and perhaps even in the USSR itself. The hopes and fears ended with the Soviet-led invasion in August, an event which both disillusioned the liberals who had hoped for reforms through the aegis of the party and state and signaled a hardening of the official line concerning dissent.[19]

Another significant transformation of the domestic political terrain occurred after Khrushchev's fall: with the issue of de-Stalinization officially laid to rest, there was now little tactical need for any leadership faction to exploit dissident themes for political advantage as Khrushchev had done in the past. In fact, the range of opinion within the new regime had considerably narrowed, and although some analysts of the 1964 to 1968 period have suggested that some high-level *apparatchiki* silently harbored the hope along with the dissidents that liberal reforms would loosen the system if not fundamentally transform it, after 1968 there seemed to be widespread agreement that stricter limitations had to be imposed. The question now, of course, was how tightly the reins would be drawn, and on that issue there was considerable vacillation, at least until 1972, when the first of a series of severe crackdowns began.[20]

While the invasion of Czechoslovakia in August, 1968, resulted in a number of protest petitions signed by leading intellectuals and university students and a brief demonstration in Red Square, this new flurry of activity was short-lived. Many of those immediately involved were subjected to "administrative penalties" such as loss of jobs or student status (which for males resulted in military service in most cases) or received the more frightful "wolf's ticket" —an entry into the permanent work record of one's dissident behavior. Predictably, over the next several years as the regime tightened controls the number of open letters and protests dropped, at least until 1971 when a new wave of protest activity emerged from the still-committed dissidents who once again had begun to organize sometimes clandestine and sometimes open groups, and who were now grimly aware of the grave risks involved. Gone, however, were both the earlier liberal hopes that the existing leadership might carry through with effective reforms and the almost carefree attitude with which some dissidents had openly criticized the system. Dissent was now a far more serious business, for both the regime and the dissidents alike.

The tone of dissent also changed in the years after the invasion of Czechoslovakia. Emphasis now fell more heavily on the critics' demands for their civil and political rights, rather than upon mere protest petitions calling for reforms, and greater stress was placed on documenting trials of dissidents and other forms of harassment in the pages of *samizdat* publications. The beginnings of a genuine philosophical dialogue between the many different schools of thought were also noted in this period, as were the first attempts to forge links between groups holding different philosophical points of view or representing different ethnic or religious groups. Increasing use was also made of foreign audiences, either through the skillful use of foreign correspondents in Moscow to channel dissident views to the West, or through direct appeals to international bodies such as the United Nations and Amnesty International.[21]

Many of the individual dissidents who were to dominate the scene throughout the next decade also became prominent in the first few years after the invasion of Czechoslovakia. Andrei Sakharov, whose reform-oriented essay *Progress, Coexistence, and Intellectual Freedom* was circulating in *samizdat* form at the time Soviet forces ousted Dubček, became a spokesman for the dissidents within the scientific community. Alexander Solzhenitsyn also moved toward an open association with other dissidents as he was increasingly frustrated by unsuccessful attempts to publish *Cancer Ward*, and as the regime's attacks on him personally and on other writers and creative artists intensified. Others such as Roy and Zhores Medvedev, Valery Chalidze, and Andrei Amalrik also emerged as highly visible critics of the regime.

Despite the increasing severity of repressive measures, the period from 1968 to 1972 saw a notable increase in the number of dissident groups. Indeed, perhaps because of the regime's harsher attitude, many of the new groups focused their attention on the protection of civil rights more than upon the advocacy of a particular point of view and gave clear evidence of a new resolve to dig in for a protracted struggle. The Initiative Group for the Defense of Human Rights was founded in 1969, and the Human Rights Committee, which was to play a leading role in focusing Western criticism on the suppression of dissidents, was created in November of 1970 with Andrei Sakharov as one of the founding members of both.[22]

The protests of Crimean Tatars and Meskhetians became more vigorous from 1969 to 1970, and the regime responded with a series of arrests and trials of major group leaders. Lithuanian Catholics also joined the ranks of active dissidents during the same period, reviving a current of mixed religious and nationality protest that had been dormant since the incorporation of the Baltic states into the USSR at the end of the war. Dissident priests within the Russian Orthodox Church also stepped up their criticism of the church hierarchy and the regime, and Baptists escalated both their public criticism of the repression of their church and clandestine efforts to conduct religious services. Without doubt, however, the most significant event in terms of ethnic and religious protest was the rapid expansion of the Jewish dissident movement. To be sure, Soviet Jews had played an important role even in earlier protest activities, in part because of their traditional concern with the protection of minority rights, and in part because of their large presence within the intelligentsia. But beginning in 1967 after the Arab-Israeli six day war, there was a surge of greater ethnic awareness among some Soviet Jews. While those who spoke out were admittedly a minority within the Jewish community itself, they became highly vocal advocates of greater latitude to practice their religion and recognize their ethnic heritage and, with increasing frequency, of the right to emigrate to Israel. Their protests continued even after the tightening of controls in 1968, when Soviet authorities resurrected anti-Semitic themes in their condemnation of both Czechoslovak reformers and Soviet dissidents. Sustained both by the intensity of their own commitment and by the support of Jewish and human rights groups abroad, they were able to win important concessions in terms of increased emigration, especially while Soviet authorities still hoped that a tacit agreement might be reached with the United States clearing the way for greater trade.[23]

From 1972 until the Helsinki Conference in 1975, increasingly severe repressive measures hit hard against a shrinking and demoralized dissident community. In December, 1971, high Soviet officials authorized the secret police to silence the *Chronicle of Current Events*, which had emerged as the focal point of dissident commentary and the most active clearing house for information about arrests and other actions against critics of the regime. The effort took fully a year and a half and was brought about only through breaking the will of key figures such as Pyotr Yakir and Viktor Krasin, whose interrogations led police to less prominent figures throughout the extensive *samizdat* network that had evolved. Even with numerous arrests, the authorities were not completely able to silence the *Chronicle* for some time: although it briefly ceased publication late in 1972, two issues were put out in 1973, four in 1974, and at least three in 1975 before the repressive measures totally took hold.[24]

From 1972 onward, the regime also turned its malevolent attention to other dissidents not directly connected with the *Chronicle*. Key figures such as Vladimir Bukovskii were incarcerated, and efforts were intensified to reach deeper into dissident circles, although with erratic results. As a consequence, large group protests and petitions became less common, although individual dissidents and a few groups such as the Initiative Group kept up the attack. Closer links among different dissident elements were also forged at this time, in part simply as the inevitable result of forming a common front against the regime, and in part in recognition that, whatever their philosophical differences, most shared the same attitudes toward basic human rights.

This period also witnessed increasingly severe attacks on Solzhenitsyn and Sakharov, who, due to the arrest or exile of other leading dissidents, were quickly emerging as the movement's most important leaders and as symbols of resistance in the eyes of foreign observers. While the fate of each will be discussed at length in later chapters, it must be noted that each surrendered whatever illusions remained about the prospects for reforms under the existing leadership. Solzhenitsyn was the first to experience the orchestrated wrath of the regime, which resulted first in an outright ban on further publication, in expulsion from the Writers' Union and inspired condemnation by fellow authors, and finally in exile from the Soviet Union in February, 1974. Sakharov survived in relative freedom until his internal exile in Gorky in January, 1980, although he too was stripped of any meaningful professional life and placed under constant surveillance in the early 1970s.[25]

In 1972 a new wave of arrests occurred among Ukrainian dissidents, who had once again become active. The Tatars and Meskhetians were less aggressive in the early 1970s, undoubtedly because the arrest of leaders in each community had taken its toll. Ethnic Germans living within the Soviet Union were the only new group to begin active dissent in this period, with their demands primarily focused on the right to emigrate. Soviet Jews also continued to press for the same opportunity, and the first half of the decade was marked both with spectacular successes such as the eventual emigration of Valery Panov and less visible victories in the growing exodus of less well known Jews, at least until the January, 1975, Soviet cancellation of an USA-USSR trade agreement because of continued American pressure for even more liberal policies.[26]

The last half of the 1970s was marked both by new initiatives on the part of hard-core dissidents who, in spite of the increasing risks, formed new protest groups and sought to broaden their base of support to include a mass audience, and by the regime's increasingly severe attempts to fragment the movement, exile its most visible leaders, and present a stoic and unflinching facade in the face of growing criticism from the West.

For the dissidents, the agreements reached by the European Security Conference, which met in Helsinki in 1975, provided a logical point of departure for intensifying their criticism of the regime. The so-called basket three accords openly agreed to by all parties provided for the maintenance of basic human rights and the greater flow of uncensored communications between East and West. Always regarded by Soviet authorities as a cosmetic necessity for the sake of achieving more important settlements in terms of an acceptance of the de facto division of Europe into spheres of influence and an improvement in East-West trade, these "basket three" standards of conduct became the major yardstick against which Soviet actions would be measured—and always found wanting. Committees of dissidents who assumed the task of monitoring Soviet compliance—the so-called Helsinki Watch Groups—came into being early in 1976, the first founded by Yuri Orlov, Yelena Bonner (Sakharov's wife), Alexander Ginzburg, Anatoly Marchenko, and Pyotr Grigorenko. Soviet authorities were quick to act, moving against the pilot Moscow group only three days after the announcement of its creation.[27] Harassment continued over the next year and intensified in the winter and spring of 1977 as the first East-West conference to evaluate the results of the accords, scheduled for that summer in Belgrade, drew closer. Orlov was himself arrested in February, 1977, and in April a concerted campaign was launched against the Ukrainian watch group. After long delays, Orlov was eventually sentenced to a harsh term of seven years imprisonment and five years in internal exile for "anti-Soviet agitation," an action that was followed rapidly by an even more severe sentence of eight years under "strict regime" handed down in July, 1978, to Alexander Ginzburg, another founder of the Moscow group.[28] Throughout 1979 trials and intensified police harassment took their toll of the remaining members of the watch groups. Until the internal exile of her husband, Andrei Sakharov, Yelena Bonner remained the only active original participant within the Moscow group, and with her departure to the isolation of Gorky, it is likely that the watch group has lost its effective voice.[29]

Another significant development in the latter half of the 1970s was the increasingly vocal reaction of the West to the suppression of dissidents in the USSR. While such protests were hardly new—American pressures concerning Jewish emigration had already resulted in the cancellation of trade agreements—they intensified during this period for a number of reasons. Exiled dissidents proved to be effective propagandists in the West in terms of mobilizing sometimes official but more often private protest campaigns in defense of their counterparts remaining in the Soviet Union. Solzhenitsyn's occasional public appearances, and his efforts to reach out to groups such as the AFL-CIO, vastly increased public awareness and stiffened both private and official criticism of Soviet actions, despite the Nixon and Ford administrations' efforts to separate the fate of détente from the treatment of dissidents and to avoid contact with dissidents in the West (a policy which produced occasional embarrassments, as with Ford's initial refusal to meet with Solzhenitsyn and the author's subsequent refusal to meet with the president on anything less than a formal basis).[30] Lesser dissident figures such as Andrei Amalrik, who had chosen voluntary exile rather than face continued harassment in the USSR, and Vladimir Bukovskii, who had been freed in a trade for the Chilean communist party leader Luis Corvalan, also took to the lecture circuit or lifted their pens in protest, and while their audiences were small, they were intensely committed to the question of human rights in the Soviet Union and always included important figures in the House and Senate who questioned the value of détente.[31]

The Carter administration's initial attention to the question of human rights also raised the level of public consciousness and escalated American verbal attacks against Soviet policies. Even though Soviet authorities objected vigorously and America's allies cautioned privately against pressing such unconventional diplomacy beyond acceptable "atmospheric" dimensions, the administration intensified its rhetorical support of the dissident movement in its first eighteen months in office, sustained both by its conviction that raising the human rights issue would not create serious roadblocks impeding progress toward SALT II, and by the urgings of dissidents themselves, who saw foreign support as important leverage against the Kremlin. While the rhetorical level of protests was toned down significantly after the summer of 1977, the basic commitment remained unaltered, even if less frequently mentioned by the president.

No such de-escalation occurred in the increasingly strident criticism which came from Congress; both the House and the Senate had quickly picked up the issue of human rights in the Soviet Union and welcomed exiled dissidents such as Solzhenitsyn to their respective chambers. Domestic groups concerned with human rights issues or the fate of their ethnic or religious counterparts in the Soviet Union also found receptive ears in Congress, and with increasing frequency from 1976 onward leading members of the House and Senate took up the cause of individual dissidents under threat of prosecution or already incarcerated in the camps or mental institutions or, as with the Jews and other ethnic minorities such as the Germans, who simply wished to emigrate.

Intensified activity by Jewish groups in the United States and Western Europe also brought additional pressures to bear on Soviet authorities. Focusing both on the fate of individual Jewish dissidents and on the broader question of the regime's restrictive emigration policies, these groups lobbied effectively for continued American insistence on free egress as a quid pro quo for improved trade, sponsored massive public demonstrations in support of Soviet Jews, and, through more militant organizations such as the Jewish Defense League, harassed Soviet diplomats and other personnel in the United States. It is difficult to assess the impact of these actions on the Soviet leadership. On the one hand, there is little to suggest that the vocal outcries of these groups alone stayed the hand of the KGB as it moved against individual Jewish dissidents, although the attention which inevitably focused on public trials of such figures may have been one of the factors that led to the greater use of exile and deprivation of Soviet citizenship in the last half of the decade. Moreover, the same period also witnessed a visible increase in the level of anti-Semitism in the USSR, embodied both in the publication of blatantly anti-Semitic tracts with tacit official sanction and in an apparently far-reaching policy of cleansing the state and party bureaucracies and the professions of high-ranking Jews, most of whom were neither active in the protest movement nor hopeful of emigration to Israel. But on the other hand, the latter half of the decade also was marked by a dramatic increase in the number of Soviet Jews permitted to leave the country; while the yearly totals fluctuated in response to the Kremlin's mood of the moment, the overall trend was toward increasing emigration, and in 1979 a record 50,000 exit visas were issued by Soviet authorities.[32] However, it is difficult to establish any clear connection between Jewish protest in the West and the easing of emigration restrictions. It is more probable that Soviet authorities manipulated departure rates in an attempt to win trade concessions or to eliminate many of the dissident movement's most vocal participants simply by permitting them to leave the country. Even though most-favored-nation status was withheld and any dramatic upsurge of trade made unlikely by continued congressional opposition, both American and Soviet officials continued to view emigration and trade as tacitly linked, at least until January, 1980, when the Carter administration embargoed grain and high-technology exports to the USSR because of the Soviet invasion of Afghanistan.

The latter half of the decade also witnessed limited attempts to carry the dissident cause either to a larger, working-class audience or to challenge the regime through the electoral process. In January, 1978, an unofficial Union for the Defense of Workers was formed in protest of the timorous conduct of the state-controlled trade union movement. Soviet authorities struck quickly, arresting the leaders in February and completing their suppression of remaining elements by the spring.[33] A short-lived effort was also made in February, 1979, to confront the regime by nominating Roy Medvedev, a leading dissident figure, and Lyudmila Agapova, another activist, to run against party-approved candidates for seats in the Supreme Soviet. While the nominations were disallowed for technical reasons, they did represent a new and probably frightening initiative in the eyes of Soviet leaders.[34]

The use of literature as a mechanism of protest once again surfaced in the winter of 1978 in connection with the open challenge of twenty-three Soviet authors—all then in favor with the Writers' Union—of the censor's decision not to publish a collection of their works entitled *Metropol*. While Solzhenitsyn had struggled in vain against controls over literature and fought a protracted battle with the censors to publish *Cancer Ward*, the issue of censorship had receded to the background after his expulsion in 1974, primarily because the leadership of the loosely coordinated dissident movement had shifted into the hands of people concerned more with political issues and with the even harsher treatment of fellow dissidents than with literary censorship per se. The protest of the *Metropol* group and the subsequent publication of the uncensored collection in the West once again raised the issue and brought the dissident literary community center stage into confrontation with the regime. Yet while Soviet authorities were quick to apply administrative sanctions such as refusals of permission to publish and a cutoff of income from translations and royalities to some of the participants, they moved with greater caution in threatening the ultimate sanction of expulsion from the Writers' Union. Only two of the lesser known figures were actually expelled, a move which quickly drew threats of voluntary resignations from the group's more prominent members. After apparently protracted backstage negotiations, a deal was struck in which the two expelled writers would be reinstated in return for a public statement deploring the "propaganda fuss of no literary relevance" that had been made about their original protest. However, last-minute resistance from conservative elements within the Writers' Union prevented the reinstatement, leading many of the original twenty-three to conclude that the regime sought their resignations and possible emigration.[35]

This seemingly vacillating and light-handed treatment of writers did not extend to other dissidents. Toward the end of the decade, Soviet authorities launched an even more strident attack against leading dissident figures. In the autumn of 1979, a new series of arrests and trials was begun, and over forty of the movement's remaining leaders were removed from the scene by the end of the year.[36] The hardest blow fell in January, 1980, with the internal exile of Andrei Sakharov, the only remaining figure who commanded the attention of a world audience. The conditions imposed in connection with his relocation to the closed city of Gorky forbad him to have direct or indirect contact with foreigners—a prohibition that he has violated on several occasions through his wife's travels to Moscow to release statements denouncing his treatment and the invasion of Afghanistan. Continuously under threat of even stricter legal sanctions and possible violence and harassed by the constantly watchful authorities, Sakharov has pledged to continue his protests and challenged the authorities to bring him to public trial.[37]

As the 1980s begin, the immediate outlook for the dissident community is grim indeed. As recently as the late 1970s, increasingly isolated leaders of the movement described themselves as "generals without armies"—and now the generals themselves have become victims of the latest encounters. Only Roy Medvedev still remains at liberty in Moscow, perhaps in large measure because he is regarded as a scholar and not an activist. But if the mood of the aging Soviet leadership has indeed hardened, and the current campaign represents a long-term commitment to silence dissidents rather than a pre-Olympics purge of leading figures or a decision to use the deterioration of Soviet-American ties as a convenient moment to strike, this still does not alter the fundamental features of contemporary Soviet society which gave rise to dissent. The complexity of the society remains, and perhaps intensifies; the "hereditary" elite is frozen in place; the malaise of a stagnant society continues; the potential for ethnic and nationality frictions grows more threatening; and, above all, the repression continues, claiming victims in the short run yet creating a pantheon of martyrs and a mythology of opposition in the longer perspective. Even the impatient Lenin counseled his followers that dramatic change could not come until the necessary groundwork had been laid and the limits of the system tested by the revolutionaries who came before with their conflicting strategies and hopes for the future. While the present generation of Soviet leaders may well succeed in stilling or exiling the now vocal spokesmen of the opposition, their successors will be forced to confront at least the causes and perhaps even the effects of such dissent.

NOTES

1. George Breslauer, "On the Adaptability of Soviet Welfare-State Authoritarianism," in *Soviet Society and the Communist Party*, ed. Karl W. Ryavec (Amherst, Mass.: University of Massachusetts Press, 1978), pp. 3–25.

2. Jerry Hough, *How the Soviet Union Is Ruled* (Cambridge, Mass.: Harvard University Press, 1978), pp. 518–55.

3. H. Gordon Skilling and Franklyn Griffiths, *Interest Groups in Soviet Politics* (Princeton, N.J.: Princeton University Press, 1971).

4. Valerie J. Bunce and John M. Echols III, "Soviet Politics in the Brezhnev Era: Pluralism or Corporatism?" in *Soviet Politics in the Brezhnev Era*, ed. Donald R. Kelley (New York: Praeger, 1980), pp. 1–26.

5. Vera S. Dunham, *In Stalin's Time: Middleclass Values in Soviet Fiction* (New York: Cambridge University Press, 1976).

6. Alexander Zinoviev, *The Yawning Heights* (New York: Random House, 1979).

7. Walter D. Conner, "Dissent in a Complex Society," *Problems of Communism* 22, no. 2 (March-April, 1973): 40–52.

8. F. J. M. Feldbrugge, *Samizdat and Political Dissent in the Soviet Union* (Leyden, Holland: Sijthoff, 1975), pp. 29–34.

9. The best studies of the early period are Abraham Rothberg, *The Heirs of Stalin: Dissidence and The Soviet Regime, 1953–1970* (Ithaca, N.Y.: Cornell University Press, 1972); and Peter Reddaway, *Uncensored Russia: Protest and Dissent in the Soviet Union* (New York: American Heritage, 1972). Studies of the 1970s include Feldbrugge, *Samizdat and Political Dissent*, George Saunders, *Samizdat: Voices of the Soviet Opposition* (New York: Monad, 1974); Rudolf L. Tokes, ed., *Dissent in the USSR: Politics, Ideology, and People* (Baltimore: Johns Hopkins University Press, 1975); Michael Meerson-Aksenov and Boris Shragin, eds., *The Political, Social, and Religious Thought of Russian "Samizdat"—An Anthology* (Belmont, Mass.: Nordland, 1977); Edward A. Corcoran, "Dissension in the Soviet Union: The Group Basis and Dynamics of Internal Opposition" (Ph.D. diss., Columbia University, 1977); and Frederick C. Barghoorn, *Detente and the Democratic Movement in the USSR* (New York: Free Press, 1976).

10. Dina Spechler, "Permitted Dissent in the Decade after Stalin, Criticism and Protest in *Novy Mir* 1955–1964," in *The Dynamics of Soviet Politics*, ed. Paul Cocks et al. (Cambridge, Mass.: Harvard University Press, 1976), pp. 28–50.

11. Boris Pasternak, *Doctor Zhivago* (New York: Pantheon, 1958).

12. Yevgeny Yevtushenko, "Stalin's Heirs," *Pravda*, 21 October 1962, p. 1.

13. Alexander I. Solzhenitsyn, *One Day in the Life of Ivan Denisovich* (New York: Praeger, 1963).

14. Corcoran, *Dissension in the Soviet Union*, pp. 48–53.

15. Ibid., pp. 53–58.

16. Ibid., pp. 58–59; and Feldbrugge, *Samizdat and Political Dissent*, pp. 110–11.

17. Alexander Ginzburg, *White Book*, cited in Feldbrugge, *Samizdat and Political Dissent*, p. 19.

18. Corcoran, *Dissension in the Soviet Union*, pp. 59–61; Reddaway, *Uncensored Russia*.

19. *See*, for example, Andrei D. Sakharov, *Progress, Coexistence, and Intellectual Freedom* (New York: Norton, 1968).

20. Corcoran, *Dissension in the Soviet Union*, pp. 62–70; Reddaway, *Uncensored Russia*; and Zhores Medvedev, *Ten Years After Ivan Denisovich* (New York: Vintage, 1974).

21. Corcoran, *Dissension in the Soviet Union*, pp. 74–80.

22. Feldbrugge, *Samizdat and Political Dissent*, p. 43.

23. Corcoran, *Dissension in the Soviet Union*, pp. 81–91; and Feldbrugge, *Samizdat and Political Dissent*, pp. 188–200.

24. Corcoran, *Dissension in the Soviet Union*, pp. 91–92.

25. For the treatment of Solzhenitsyn, *see* Medvedev, *Ten Years*, and Solzhenitsyn, *The Oak and the Calf* (New York: Harper and Row, 1980). For Sakharov's treatment, *see* his *My Country and the World* (New York: Vintage, 1975), and *Alarm and Hope* (New York: Vintage, 1978).

26. Corcoran, *Dissension in the Soviet Union*, p. 97.

27. *New York Times*, 14 May 1976, p. 1, and 16 May 1976, p. 3.

28. *New York Times*, 19 May 1978, p. 3, and 14 July 1978, p. 1.

29. *New York Times*, 23 January 1980, p. 1.

30. *New York Times*, 22 July 1975, p. 1, and 23 July 1975, p. 7.

31. Concerning Amalrik, *see New York Times*, 13 April 1976, p. 3; and concerning Bukovskii, *see New York Times*, 18 December 1976, p. 1.

32. *New York Times*, 10 October 1978, p. 18, 4 March 1979, p. 1, 4 May 1979, p. 3, and 27 June 1979, p. 2.

33. *New York Times*, 11 January 1978, p. 4, 15 January 1978, IV p. 20, 27 January 1978, p. 2, 8 February 1978, p. 7, and 28 February 1978, p. 7.

34. *New York Times*, 3 February 1979, p. 2, and 18 February 1979, p. 8.

35. *New York Times*, 20 December 1979, p. 3.

36. *New York Times*, 17 January 1980, p. 3, and 27 January 1980, IV p. 2.

37. *New York Times*, 23 January 1980, p. 1, 25 January 1980, p. 9, 5 February 1980, p. 9, and 11 February 1980, p. 8.

2

Alexander I. Solzhenitsyn: An Intellectual Biography

*Fate was not seeking its victim: the victim had set out
to meet his fate.*

The Oak and the Calf

The outlines of that fate were far from apparent in Solzhenitsyn's early years. He was born on December 11, 1918, in Kislovodsk, the son of a former university student who had terminated his studies in the Department of Philology at Moscow State University to enlist in the army, only to be killed in the summer of that year six months before his son's birth. Raised by his mother, who worked as a typist and stenographer in Rostov-on-the-Don, Solzhenitsyn excelled as a student, completing secondary school in 1936. During his youth, he "experienced an entirely unprompted inclination toward writing" and produced a "great deal of the usual adolescent nonsense," which the author sought in vain to publish throughout the 1930s.[1]

The literary education that Solzhenitsyn had hoped to pursue proved unavailable in the still-provincial Rostov, and the family's modest income and his mother's illness prevented him from journeying to Moscow. Instead Solzhenitsyn entered Rostov University with a prestigious Stalin Scholarship to study mathematics, a subject he easily mastered and that, by his own account, saved his life on two occasions—once in the assignment to the *sharashka* after his arrest and again in providing employment after his release from the camps. Yet the desire to study literature continued, and concurrently with his studies of mathematics and physics, he took correspondence courses from the Institute of History, Philosophy, and Literature in Moscow. By the completion of his university training in 1941, Solzhenitsyn had firmly decided to devote himself to literature despite the more lucrative opportunities open to a skilled mathmetician.[2] The author's own thoughts about his education and intended role are spoken by the surrogate Gleb Nerzhin in *First Circle:*

Young Gleb had grown up in that city. From the cornucopia of science, success was showered upon him. He found out that his mind worked quickly, but that there were others whose minds worked even faster, whose wealth of knowledge oppressed him. The People remained on the book shelves; he was convinced that the only people who matter are those who carry in their heads the accumulated culture of the world, encyclopedists, connoisseurs of antiquity, men who value beauty; highly educated, many-sided men. *One must belong to that elite.*[3] (Emphasis added.)

The outbreak of war cut short Solzhenitsyn's immediate hopes for a literary career and cast him instead into the army, where he initially served throughout the winter of 1941-42 in a horse-drawn transport unit, a frustrating experience which forcefully reminded him of the practical incompetence of the intelligentsia. He was later transferred to artillery school, where he completed an abridged course of study in November, 1942, and then was placed in command of an observation battery in which he served continuously until his arrest in February, 1945.[4]

Retrospectively viewing his brief military career from the camps some years later, Solzhenitsyn recoiled from the ease with which he succumbed to "the happiness of simplification, of being a military man and not having to think things through" and to the temptation of exploiting the perquisites of rank. Yet as an officer and a unit commander, Solzhenitsyn soon convinced himself that he was "a superior human being," whose treatment of his subordinates was no less exacting and harsh than others who had earned their officer's epaulets and carefully rehearsed their "tigerlike stride and . . . metallic voice of command."[5] But even in those years, he continued to write short stories and reflections on his military service which he carried in his field bag.

At the time of Solzhenitsyn's arrest in early 1945, Soviet Russia was already deep in the throes of a sweeping campaign to restore discipline and ferret out potential disloyalty. Particular attention was focused on the military, especially those units that had served abroad, although no segment of society was immune from suspicion. As surveillance intensified near the end of the war, military censors monitoring Solzhenitsyn's correspondence with a friend noted what the author terms "certain disrespectful remarks" about the *Vozhd*, and this was sufficient to prompt his arrest.[6] These comments, plus the moderately critical manuscripts found in the author's field bag, led one of the then-proliferating Special Commissions of the NKVD to sentence Solzhenitsyn to eight years of internment, which was then considered a mild sentence.

The years in prison were both a trial and a rebirth for Solzhenitsyn. In comparison with other prisoners, Solzhenitsyn's lot was bearable and at times relatively comfortable, at least in the physical sense. For those victims of Stalin's postwar purges who were swept into the camps at a later time, a ten year, and then twenty-five year term became the norm. For the first year of his incarceration, Solzhenitsyn served in a corrective labor camp, working mostly in the construction industry rebuilding parts of the capital itself. In 1946, he was transferred to a *sharashka*, a prisoner-staffed research institute such as that described in *First Circle* in which the author's mathematical training was utilized by the perversely logical prison system. In 1950, he was reassigned to the new "special" camps which housed only political prisoners; in such a camp in Ekibastuz in Kazakhstan he worked as a common laborer, a bricklayer, and a foundryman until he developed a malignant tumor, which was incorrectly treated in the prison hospital.[7]

Despite the hardships, the years in prison were also a period of rebirth. Prison provided not only the time to think but also the harsh and exacting trials through which Solzhenitsyn's character and attitudes were formed. Speaking again through his surrogate,

Gleb Nerzhin, he exalts in his confinement: "Thank God for prison! It gave me time to think."[8] He then adds:

. . . Nerzhin was secretly happy in that unhappiness. He drank it down like spring water. Here he got to know people and events about which he could learn nowhere else on earth, certainly not in the quiet, well-fed seclusion of the domestic hearth. From his youth on, Gleb Nerzhin had dreaded more than anything else wallowing in daily living. As the proverb says: "It's not the sea that drowns you, it's the puddle."[9]

The transfer from the *sharashka* to the more demanding general labor camp at Ekibastuz further cemented the new character in place, although Solzhenitsyn initially was apprehensive:

I was anxious and unsure of myself to begin with. Could I keep it up? We were unhandy cerebral creatures, and the same amount of work was harder for us than for our teammates. But the day when I deliberately let myself sink to the bottom and felt it firm under my feet—the hard, rocky bottom which is the same for all—was the beginning of the most important years of my life, the years which put the finishing touches on my character. From then onward . . . I have been faithful to the views and habits acquired at that time.[10]

The years in prison also brought a new spiritual awareness and a conversion to Christianity. While as a youth Solzhenitsyn had evidently been affected by religion—in a letter to the patriarch, he speaks of a "childhood of attending many church services" which formed a "uniquely fresh and pure first impression which could not later be obliterated by any of life's hardships or by any abstract intellectual theories"[11]—he did not formally undergo baptism until after his release in 1953. Even more importantly, his spiritual conversion while still buried deep in Gulag gave Solzhenitsyn the conviction that his fate was somehow being guided by forces outside of himself, by some greater "Absolute" which, in later years, informs and gives structure to a system of values and imperatives which are the ethical core of his political and social philosophy. As early as his arrest in 1945, he sensed the presence of such a "guiding hand" that fated him, through his writings, to affect the history of his homeland.[12]

As a part of this spiritual awakening, Solzhenitsyn came to believe in the existence of an innate and absolute "internal moral law,"[13] alogical in nature, which gives meaning and structure to his concept of ethics. From such ethics "all relationships, fundamental principles, and laws flow directly."[14] Thus justice is a concept which is inherent and absolute. "There is nothing relative about justice," he argues in his "Letter to Three Students," "just as there is nothing relative about conscience."[15] The "Absolute" exists independently of man and is knowable only through intuition and revelation, but not through the application of rational thought. The evolution of society is likewise regarded as a fulfillment of some more grandiose and dimly perceived scheme. "History is irrational . . . ," insists a character in *August 1914*, "It has its own, and to us perhaps incomprehensible, organic structure."[16] In such a milieu, the task of each person is to develop his soul, to "preserve unspoiled, undisturbed, and undistorted the image of eternity with which each person is born."[17]

The years in prison also provided the *raison d'être* for Solzhenitsyn's struggle for survival: to recount the story of the horrors of Gulag, to speak for "those millions who did not write, whisper, or even gasp out the story of their imprisonment, their last testament from the camps."[18] Convinced that "my literary destiny was not just my own affair," Solzhenitsyn honed his writing skills in the camps, painfully destroying his precious drafts and committing his verses and short passages to memory when possible.[19] He also sought out the histories of other unfortunates, compiling the chronicle of repression, cowardice, determination, and occasional defiance that comprises the Gulag volumes.

Yet it would be inaccurate to suggest that the years in prison brought the first awakening of Solzhenitsyn's political consciousness. While these years hardened his resolve and provided an appropriate genre for the expression of his outrage—"I hate to think what sort of writer I would have become . . . ," he comments in *The Oak and the Calf*, "if I had not been *put inside*"[20]—the realization that Stalin's Russia was based on lies and repression came early in adolescence. Once again the surrogate Gleb Nerzhin, who had "since adolescence been hearing a mute bell," speaks for the author:

. . . at the age of twelve, he had gone through an enormous pile of *Izvestiia* as tall as he was and he had read about the trial of the saboteur engineers. From the very first, the boy did not believe what he had read. He did not know why . . . but he could clearly see that it was all a lie.[21]

And later:

Gleb was only a ninth-grader on the December morning when he looked into a display window where a newspaper was posted and read that Kirov had been killed. And suddenly, like a blinding light, it became clear to him that Stalin and no one else had killed Kirov.[22]

For the youth, the impact of this discovery was decisive:

For Gleb Nerzhin the mute bell thundered through his entire youth. An inviolable decision took root in him: to learn and understand! To learn and understand! Strolling the boulevards of his native city when it would have been more fitting to sigh over a girl, Gleb went around dreaming of the day when he would sort everything out and would, perhaps, even penetrate within the walls where those people [the victims of the purges], as one, had vilified themselves before they died. Perhaps inside those walls it could be understood.[23]

Hardened and given purpose by events "inside those walls," Solzhenitsyn welcomed his release from the camps in March, 1953, both as a personal liberation and as the beginning of his new life as a writer. He was initially restricted to the small village of Kok-Terek in southern Kazakhstan for three additional years of "administrative exile." Soon after his release, his incorrectly treated tumor developed rapidly, bringing him to the brink of death by the end of 1953. He sought treatment in the oncological clinic in Tashkent and ministered to himself with various folk remedies, and by the end of the following year was once again able to return to his duties as a teacher of mathematics and physics at the local school. Clandestinely he wrote "for the drawer," concealing his manuscripts and even the fact that he wrote at all from his associates. In June, 1956, he was permitted to return to the European part of the country, where he continued both his teaching and secret literary pursuits, first near Vladimir and then in Ryazan.[24]

Four months before Solzhenitsyn's return to European Russia, the Twentieth Party Congress began the traumatic process of de-Stalinization. For the wiley Khrushchev, who had launched a carefully tailored frontal assault on the former dictator through his so-called secret speech, the denunciation was meant both as a tactical ploy against his conservative enemies within the Presidium and as an honest, if incompletely thought out, attempt to set the stage for meaningful reforms. The relevations about the crimes of the Stalin era and the deleterious consequences of the "personality cult" were meant to condemn through association those high-ranking lieutenants of Stalin who now opposed the newly liberal First Secretary's reform proposals. For both Khrushchev's entourage and the intended victims of the de-Stalinization campaign, the political ramifications were immediately apparent, and the First Secretary's opponents were quick to join the battle, winning some impressive victories until they overplayed their hand in the abortive coup attempt in June, 1957. Yet even with his victory over the "antiparty group," as the plotters were pejoratively labeled, Khrushchev was unable to consolidate his hold over his erstwhile supporters. At both the Twenty-First Extraordinary Party Congress in 1959 and the Twenty-Second Party Congress in 1961, Khrushchev revived the de-Stalinization issue as a partisan weapon, and on both occasions his forays against Stalin's "heirs" met with only limited success.

Even though Solzhenitsyn had been cleared retroactively of all charges in 1957 and awarded full civil rights, as had many other former prisoners after 1956, it was not until after the Twenty-Second Party Congress in 1961, which launched the most vigorous attack on the Stalinist past, that he chose to seek publication through the officially approved channels. By the author's own account, the frustrations of secret authorship and the absence of intelligent criticism of his works had begun to weigh upon him, and at the age of forty-two, he decided upon the risky venture of sending a self-censored version of *One Day in The Life of Ivan Denisovich* to the liberal *Novy Mir*, edited by Alexander Tvardovskii.[25] Realizing both the manuscript's potential in terms of challenging the existing parameters set forth by the censors, and its possible political usefulness to Khrushchev, Tvardovskii brought it to the attention of the First Secretary through one of his aides. After a year of delay and indecision, publication was finally approved.[26]

Solzhenitsyn's contact with *Novy Mir* also brought about an uneasy alliance between Tvardovskii and the author. In the first several years after his emergence as a public figure, Solzhenitsyn continued to hope that his works would be published within the Soviet Union. As a consequence, he adopted a tactical stance of limited cooperation with establishment figures such as Tvardovskii, who were no less interested in challenging the censors, but who were also bound by their acceptance of the Soviet form of government and Marxist dogma, views long since discarded by the author. Even as Solzhenitsyn and Tvardovskii wrangled over new manuscripts such as *The First Circle* or the theatrical performance of *Candle in the Wind* and *The Love Girl and the Innocent*, the political milieu around them became perceptibly less receptive to further liberalization.[27] Khrushchev himself now approved stricter controls, and the book form of *One Day* quickly disappeared from library shelves. Solzhenitsyn quickly soured on his former benefactor, confessing years later in the *Gulag Archipelago* that "I (even I!) succumbed, and I do not deserve forgiveness. . . . I, too, genuinely believed that the story [*One Day*] I had brought him was about the past!"[28] But the real awakening came from letters surreptitiously sent by present-day prisoners, all with a "single many-throated cry . . . a cry that said: 'What about us!!??' . . . 'Nothing has changed since Ivan Denisovich's time'—the message was the same in letters from many different places."[29] "And so," concludes Solzhenitsyn, "I came to my senses. And through the pink perfumed clouds of rehabilitation I could make out the familiar rocky piles of the Archipelago, its gray outlines broken by watchtowers."[30]

Khrushchev's removal from power set the stage for a hardening of cultural policy in general, although the first public action against errant writers, the arrest of Sinyavskii and Daniel, was delayed until a year after his fall. Solzhenitsyn's initial reaction to the coup against Khrushchev was mixed. On the one hand, he was concerned that the First Secretary's demise possibly foreshadowed his own repression, and he sought unsuccessfully to withdraw the controversial *First Circle* from consideration for publication and substitute the less explosive *Cancer Ward* in its place, hoping to pass the change off as merely a retitling of the same work.[31] But on the other hand, Solzhenitsyn also regarded Khrushchev's removal as a liberation from a debt of honor to the political figure who had first, albeit temporarily, championed his cause; now freed of this debt and increasingly skeptical that Tvardovskii had the stern will needed for a protracted conflict with the newly conservative regime, Solzhenitsyn stiffened his own resolve against any future "tactical" concessions for publication of his works within Russia and against the suggestions of more moderate figures such as Tvardovskii that he produce a few acceptable publications to allay the fears of the regime. Still cautiously aware of the delicacy of his position, he remained silent concerning the conviction of Sinyavskii and Daniel, hoping to "vanish into the depths" to continue writing. But his attempt to escape the attention of the regime failed, and he fell into a period a depression and inactivity after the seizure by the KGB of copies of some of his most controversial works, including *The Feast of the Victors* and *The First Circle*, late in 1965.[32]

In 1966, he emerged from a brief period of depression even more resolved to struggle publicly with the regime. Reasoning that with his existing works already in the hands of the secret police he had little to lose, Solzhenitsyn began to grant interviews and seek a public audience for his criticism. He read sections of the unpublished *Cancer Ward* to select audiences and lectured on the repressiveness of the censors, his lectures both electrifying his audiences and confounding the KGB, which had expected anything but bold defiance. Solzhenitsyn gloried in the new activism, finding in it justifications for his suffering:

Yes, I was beginning to enjoy the new position in which the loss of my records had left me! To enjoy my proud and open defiance, my acknowledged right to think for myself! It would, I daresay, have been painful, perhaps impossible, to return to my previous quiet life. At last I was beginning to see revealed the higher and hidden meaning of that suffering for which I had been unable to find a justification. . . . This was why my murderous misfortunes had been sent to me—to deny me all possibility, snatch from me any chance of lying low and keeping quiet, to make me desperate enough to speak and act.

For the time was at hand. . . . [33]

Solzhenitsyn's first major attack was launched in May, 1967, in his "Open Letter to the Fourth Congress of the Writers' Union," which demanded that censorship be ended and that the union vigorously defend its members against repression. He returned to the offensive against the still silent union in September, challenging it to refute an officially inspired campaign of gossip against him and to authorize publication of *Cancer Ward*.[34] Summoned to defend his actions and this controversial volume before union officials, Solzhenitsyn held his ground, noting the joy—and the unexpected success—of standing firm before the authorities. By January of the following year, however, Tvardovskii's *Novy Mir* was forced to abandon its hopes to publish *Cancer Ward* domestically, and within a month an edition was published in Italy, evidently spirited there by a KGB operative in the hope of inculpating Solzhenitsyn for slander of the Soviet state, a criminal offense. The even more damning *First Circle* was published in Germany in June of 1968, although the author denied any responsibility for its release in the West.[35]

The Soviet-led invasion of Czechoslovakia in August, 1968, even more firmly convinced Solzhenitsyn that any hope for internal reform was impossible. Pressure against all dissidents subsequently intensified, and the liberal Tvardovskii's days at the head of *Novy Mir* were obviously numbered. Although he entertained the notion of circulating a petition critical of the Soviet invasion among the most prominent scientific and cultural figures, Solzhenitsyn canceled his plans at the last moment, retreating into a despairing and guilt-ridden silence since the Prague spring itself had begun with a leading Czech liberal reading Solzhenitsyn's letter to the Writers' Union to a similar gathering within his own country.[36]

Soviet authorities made the next move, interrupting the author's attempt to maintain a low profile in order to continue writing in November, 1969, with a summons to appear before the miniscule seven-member Ryazan branch of the Writers' Union. Still officially a member of this provincial branch because of his previous residence there, Solzhenitsyn struggled in vain against the *fait accompli* that awaited him—expulsion from the Writers' Union, a measure that deprived him of any lingering hope of publication within the USSR. Now stripped of his "official" status as a writer and increasingly the subject of Western interest and commentary—the expulsion was reported in the Western press and on the BBC and Voice of America even before the action of the Ryazan branch was confirmed by central authorities in Moscow—Solzhenitsyn briefly went on the offensive with a strongly worded attack against the Secretariat of the Writers' Union of the Russian Republic.[37] Once again stunned by the audacity of the writer's open challenge, the authorities withheld any overt response, although surveillance was increased. Solzhenitsyn returned to his writing tasks in the respite that followed, now the guest of Mstislav Rostropovich, who had invited him to stay in his country estate in the closed residence area of Zhukovka, less than twenty miles from Moscow.[38] During the spring and summer of 1970, official harassment intensified, and it was rumored that Soviet authorities were planning his expulsion from the country by year's end.[39]

Solzhenitsyn's Nobel Prize, awarded in October, 1970, upset the authorities' plans and catapulted the author even more into the attention of the West. For Solzhenitsyn, the award came at a propitious moment in his struggle with the regime; now increasingly on the defensive because of the harassment and rumormongering of the authorities, he badly needed a rostrum from which to speak. Although he was prepared to strike out even without such a ready-made forum, he initially welcomed the prize, cautious only to arrange for the presentation and the public release of his Nobel lecture in some fashion that permitted him to remain within his homeland. The likelihood that Soviet authorities would bar his return from the awards ceremony, and the unwillingness of

Swedish authorities to risk offending their Soviet counterparts, caused Solzhenitsyn to sour on the proceedings; he remained at home, outraged that a presentation ceremony could not be arranged at that time within the Swedish embassy in Moscow and that his message to the awards banquet in Stockholm had been censored by nervous Nobel authorities.[40]

Following the Nobel "fiasco," as he termed it, Solzhenitsyn lapsed into a period of inactivity and depression. Long estranged from his first wife and residing with Natalya Svetlova, who was soon to bear him a son, Solzhenitsyn finally undertook legal divorce proceedings and formally wed Svetlova, steps that he had postponed for several years because of preoccupation with his work. While he soon returned to his writing desk at the Rostropovich estate to continue work on *August 1914*, he avoided overt political activity. Admitting that the "steel-hard resolve with which I had hacked my way through the years since my arrest, and without which I would never reach my goal, had softened somewhat," Solzhenitsyn devoted himself to his writing and to ingenious means of spiriting his manuscripts to safety in the West, justifying his silence by arguing that he was "planning and timing actions far ahead."[41]

With his works now in what he thought were safe hands, Solzhenitsyn once again returned to the offensive. His open letter "To Patriarch Pimen of Russia" and the *Nobel Lecture*, first published in August, 1972, after Swedish authorities finally agreed to a presentation ceremony in their embassy in Moscow, again brought the wrath of Soviet authorities down upon him. In the autumn of 1972, Solzhenitsyn once more withdrew to his writing tasks, completing work on another "knot" of the historical epic of World War I and the revolution and failing to protest the harsh sanctions imposed on other leading dissidents.[42]

The summer and autumn of 1973 brought what Solzhenitsyn terms an "encounter battle"—a confrontation in which both sides simultaneously decide to attack and unexpectedly collide. For his part, Solzhenitsyn was animated both by the desire to pursue what he describes as the "cascade strategy" in which a flurry of attacks launched in quick succession stun and overwhelm the enemy, leaving the aggressor a breathing space in which to pursue his own goals, and by the seizure of a copy of the *Gulag Archipelago*. His immediate response to the latter was to order the publication of *Gulag* in the West, and on the same day he passed these instructions to his representative in Switzerland, he posted his *Letter to the Soviet Leaders*. Originally he had intended this combination indictment and programmatic statement to be a "deafening thunderclap," but his wife convinced him to soften its strident tones in "the infinitesimal hope that they would heed it instead of instantly dismissing it as propaganda; let them think quietly!"[43]

Soviet authorities also launched an intensified campaign against dissidents in the summer and autumn of 1973. Striking hardest at the so-called democratic movement and its most visible proponent, Andrei Sakharov, they initiated a new wave of arrests and a vigorous press campaign against Solzhenitsyn and Sakharov. For his part, Solzhenitsyn let Sakharov take the lead in responding to their critics, arguing that "my battle was ahead, my strength, every ounce of it, would yet be needed."[44] The two met only once during the entire period, and no effort was made to coordinate their actions, although Solzhenitsyn did show Sakharov a copy of his soon to be published Nobel lecture and nominated him for a Nobel Prize in his own right. By the late autumn, the campaign against dissidents waned, due as much to the surprisingly active response of the West—a response that Solzhenitsyn had earlier discounted—and to a recognition by Soviet authorities that the dissidents themselves could not easily be cowed into silence.[45]

The remainder of the year passed in tense silence; now removed from the calming surroundings of the Rostropovich estate to his wife's apartment in Moscow, Solzhenitsyn contemplated the future not only with a sense of apprehension—surely the regime would retaliate in some fashion for the upcoming publication of *Gulag Archipelago* in the West, but how, and when?—but also with a feeling of resolution and strength. The battle would soon be joined, he reasoned, for Sakharov and his wife were once again the victims of a now silent campaign of harassment that would quickly encompass others. "In my life," Solzhenitsyn concluded, "this is the great moment, the struggle, perhaps the reason why I have lived at all."[46]

But when the regime acted in December, 1973, it approached first with an olive branch rather than a cudgel. Using Solzhenitsyn's former wife as the intermediary, Soviet authorities offered a tacit deal: limited publication of a presumably edited version of *Cancer Ward* within the Soviet Union in return for a period of silence on his part and some visible disassociation from the political uses of his works in the West. Solzhenitsyn rejected the offer out of hand, interpreting it as a sign of indecision and weakness on the part of the authorities.[47]

In the last nervous months before his exile, Solzhenitsyn busied himself with the assembly of *From Under the Rubble*, a collection of essays by himself and other dissidents that, more clearly than previous writings, revealed his concept of Russian nationalism and his debt to the prerevolutionary thinkers who contributed to *Vechi*.[48] Acknowledging that *Vechi* spoke of "our own times" as well as of the past, Solzhenitsyn and the other authors of *From Under the Rubble* condemn the present Soviet intelligentsia and much of the dissident movement for ignoring the uniquely and inherently Russian features of the milieu within which they operate.[49] To be Russian, the authors contend, is to internalize and manifest the cultural, linguistic, and ethnic essence of the Russian experience, which is expressed in literature and art and, less directly, in social custom. Like history itself, it is beyond logic and rationality; it is an act of communion and faith, not calculation and decision. To be sure, some of Solzhenitsyn's earlier writings had expressed these notions in embryonic form. The surrogate Gleb Nerzhin had found his own definition of "the people" in his trials in the camps, and other figures such as the groundskeeper in *Zakhar-the-Pouch* had exemplified elements of this "Russianness."[50] But with the emergence of *From Under the Rubble*, the element of Russian nationalism, uniquely defined in cultural and psychological terms, became a central and clearly articulated factor in Solzhenitsyn's thinking.

Shortly after the new year, Soviet authorities responded bitterly to the publication of *Gulag* in the West. Solzhenitsyn once again became the target of a campaign of vilification in the media, and his personal safety and that of members of his family were repeatedly threatened. Wishing to make it clear that he would hold his ground undaunted, he delayed publication of the *Letter to the Soviet Leaders*, which he thought might be interpreted as a conciliatory gesture because of what he regarded as its studied, moderate tone; instead he intended that it be paired at a later date with the strongly worded *Live Not by Lies*, a more recent and more strident indictment.[51]

On February 12, 1974, the blow finally fell. Seized late in the afternoon by KGB agents at his apartment, Solzhenitsyn was taken to Lefortovo Prison and initially threatened with indictment for treason under the provisions of Article 64 of the criminal code. Reviewing events that sleepless night, the author for the first time regretted not having taken the opportunity to leave the country in 1970, in connection with the Nobel Prize. And as Solzhenitsyn pondered his fate, his wife and friends burned letters and documents in their Moscow apartment, while others, including Sakharov, manned protests and vigils at the prison and the office of the Procuracy. The following day, prosecution under Article 64 seemed less likely—Solzhenitsyn speculates that the KGB hoped that the ruse would force him to seek concessions—and rumors swept the dissident community and its Western contacts that he would be stripped of his Soviet citizenship and expelled. By early afternoon of the thirteenth, Solzhenitsyn was aboard a special plane en route to the Federal Republic of Germany and his first day of the expatriation as a guest of the German writer Heinrich Böll, his wife and child soon to follow. And as he left his homeland, he carried in his pocket a crust of bread from the Lefortovo ration, like Ivan Denisovich marching from the camp to survive yet another day.[52]

Solzhenitsyn's reception in the West was tumultuous; welcomed more as a conqueror than an exile, he initially withdrew into a period of cautious silence, as much to avoid the clamoring Western media as to plan his own future. He eventually settled on a rural estate in Cavendish, Vermont, a setting which reminded him of his native land, where he has continued work on the "knots" of his epic of war and revolution. With all restrictions now lifted, he began to pen even more vigorous attacks on the Soviet system. *From Under the Rubble*, which had been completed shortly before the author's exile, was published in the West, and *Letter to the*

Soviet Leaders was released for publication. Even more importantly, Solzhenitsyn personally carried his message to Congress—although not to a nervous Ford administration, which refused to meet with him—and to the public in general. And as he sought a wider audience in the West, Solzhenitsyn's gaze inevitably fell upon his new homeland. Critical of the West even before his exile, he now vigorously spoke out against its alleged decadence and its lack of resolution in the struggle with totalitarian systems. Both in *Warning to the West* and his Harvard commencement address, later published as *A World Split Apart*, he prophesied the eventual fall of the West and condemned the liberal and humanist traditions that allegedly have sapped its strength, positions that have cost him considerable support within the Western intelligentsia.[53] Now seen by Western audiences as much as a political figure—although it is a designation he continues to reject—as a novelist of Tolstoian proportions, Solzhenitsyn has increasingly identified with conservative and traditionally anti-Soviet institutions and causes. His strident criticism of liberal democracy and Western culture, and his insistence on morality and ethics as the touchstones of national and international affairs first confused and then irritated Western commentators. Solzhenitsyn's unbending defense of the uniqueness and, implicitly, the inherent superiority of the Russian experience, as well as his propensity to sally forth from the seclusion of the Cavendish estate to issue sweeping Delphic pronouncements, have added to the impression that there is something vaguely anachronistic about the man and his views. No less a figure than Norman Cousins has concluded that "he may be a man speaking to the wrong century,"[54] and others have written him off as a twentieth-century Slavophile,[55] or a self-centered recluse who does not understand those aspects of Western culture that he condemns out of hand.[56] Yet such attempts to deal with the man and his philosophy simply as expressions of another age or a distant culture miss the reality that Solzhenitsyn, however strange his vocabulary to Western ears, speaks to the central issue extant in defining the complex interplay of history, culture, and social institutions in any modern society. That his particular *Weltanschauung* stresses traditional cultural values and an absolutist sense of morality and ethics as the central, integrating features of society is consistent with his view that ultimately societies, like individual men, bear a unique and divinely inspired essence.

NOTES

1. Alexander I. Solzhenitsyn, *"Autobiography"* [writen for Nobel Committee], (Stockholm: Nobel Foundation, 1971), reprinted in *Alexandr Solzhenitsyn: Critical Essays and Documentary Materials*, eds. John B. Dunlop, Richard Haugh, and Alexis Klimoff, 2d ed. (New York: Collier, 1975), pp. 537–40.

2. Ibid.

3. Alexander I. Solzhenitsyn, *The First Circle* (New York: Harper and Row, 1968), pp. 234–35.

4. Solzhenitsyn, *Autobiography*.

5. Alexander I. Solzhenitsyn, *The Gulag Archipelago*, vols. 1–2 (New York: Harper and Row, 1973), pp. 163–64.

6. Solzhenitsyn, *Autobiography*.

7. Ibid. *See also* David Burg and George Feifer, *Solzhenitsyn* (New York: Stein and Day, 1972), pp. 75–99.

8. Solzhenitsyn, *First Circle*, p. 33.

9. Ibid., pp. 156–57.

10. Alexander I. Solzhenitsyn, *The Gulag Archipelago*, vols. 5–7 (New York: Harper and Row, 1978), p. 98.

11. Alexander I. Solzhenitsyn, "To Patriarch Pimen of Russia," reprinted in Dunlop, Haugh, and Klimoff, *Alexander Solzhenitsyn*, pp. 550–55.

12. Alexander I. Solzhenitsyn, *The Oak and the Calf: Sketches of Literary Life in the Soviet Union* (New York: Harper and Row, 1980), p. 4.

13. Alexander I. Solzhenitsyn, *Candle in the Wind* (New York: Bantam, 1974), pp. 118–19.

14. Alexander I. Solzhenitsyn, *Cancer Ward* (New York: Farrar, Straus, and Giroux, 1969), p. 442.

15. Alexander I. Solzhenitsyn, "Letter to Three Students," reprinted in Leopold Labadz, *Solzhenitsyn: A Documentary Record* (Bloomington, Ind.: Indiana University Press, 1973), pp. 151–52.

16. Alexander I. Solzhenitsyn, *August 1917* (New York: Farrar, Straus, and Giroux, 1972), pp. 409–10.

17. Solzhenitsyn, *Cancer Ward*, p. 428.

18. Solzhenitsyn, *Oak and the Calf*, p. 4.

19. Ibid.
20. Ibid., p. 2.
21. Solzhenitsyn, *First Circle*, pp. 202-4.
22. Ibid.
23. Ibid.; Compare the elements of the fictional Gleb's account with the author's comments in *Gulag Archipelago*, vols. 5-7, p. 21: "I was keenly interested in politics from the age of ten; even as a callow adolescent I did not believe Vyshinsky and was staggered by the fraudulence of the famous trials."
24. Solzhenitsyn, *Autobiography*.
25. Ibid.
26. Burg and Feifer, *Solzhenitsyn*, pp. 147-65.
27. Solzhenitsyn, *Oak and the Calf*, pp. 50-67.
28. Solzhenitsyn, *Gulag Archipelago*, vols. 5-7, p. 476.
29. Ibid., pp. 477-78.
30. Ibid., p. 479.
31. Solzhenitsyn, *Oak and the Calf*, pp. 88-92.
32. Ibid., pp. 101-2.
33. Ibid., p. 146.
34. Ibid., pp. 139-40.
35. Ibid., pp. 204-7.
36. Ibid., p. 222.
37. Ibid., pp. 257-70.
38. Ibid., p. 270.
39. Burg and Feifer, *Solzhenitsyn*, p. 312.
40. Solzhenitsyn, *Oak and the Calf*, pp. 292-303; Ibid., p. 329.
41. Solzhenitsyn, *Oak and the Calf*, p. 312.
42. Ibid., pp. 328-34.
43. Ibid., pp. 350-51.
44. Ibid., p. 351.
45. Ibid., p. 352.
46. Ibid., p. 378.
47. Ibid., pp. 360-66.
48. Ibid., pp. 388-89.
49. Alexander I. Solzhenitsyn, et al., *From Under the Rubble* (Boston: Little, Brown, 1975), p. 230.
50. Solzhenitsyn, *First Circle*, pp. 386-89, and "Zakhar-the-Pouch," in Alexander Solzhenitsyn, *Stories and Prose Poems* (New York: Bantam, 1972), pp. 107-21; *see also* Stephen Carter, *The Politics of Solzhenitsyn* (New York: Holmes and Meier, 1977), pp. 62-63.

51. Solzhenitsyn, *Oak and the Calf*, pp. 383–97.

52. Ibid., pp. 410–43.

53. Alexander I. Solzhenitsyn, *Warning to the West* (New York: Farrar, Straus, and Giroux, 1976); idem, *A World Split Apart* (New York: Harper and Row, 1978).

54. Norman Cousins, "Brief Encounter with A. Solzhenitsyn," *Saturday Review*, 23 August 1975, pp. 4–8.

55. Carter, *Politics of Solzhenitsyn*, pp. 141–47. Actually, the proper term is a proponent of the "native soil movement."

56. Hans J. Morganthau, "What Solzhenitsyn Doesn't Understand," *The New Leader*, 3 July 1978, pp. 12–13.

3

Alexander I. Solzhenitsyn and the Traditional Moral Order

Alexander Solzhenitsyn is undoubtedly better known to Western audiences than is Andrei Sakharov, both for his unquestioned contribution to world literature and for his dramatic expulsion from the Soviet Union. Himself a victim of the Stalinist labor camps after the war, Solzhenitsyn has offered a chilling view of this system in his semifictional works *One Day in the Life of Ivan Denisovitch* and *The First Circle*, and in his documentary *Gulag Archipelago*.[1] Blending his semiautobiographical accounts of personal experiences in the camps with the combined recollections of other victims, he has created a damning factual narrative and moral condemnation that has dominated the genre of camp literature since it first came into being in the 1960s.[2]

It is to other works, however, that the reader must turn for an understanding of Solzhenitsyn's political and social philosophy and his hope for the evolutionary development of Russia. Of principal importance are essays such as the *Letter to the Soviet Leaders* and *Nobel Lecture*, his contributions in *From Under the Rubble*, his 1978 Harvard commencement address, and a collection of speeches and interviews published as *Warning to the West*.[3] In these works the image of Solzhenitsyn as a literary figure recedes and there emerges the profile of a man profoundly concerned about the impact of Western culture and technology, the uncritical desire for ill-defined "progress," and the moral and spiritual crises of industrial society, and instead determined to redefine and rebuild society on the basis of traditional cultural values.

Letter to the Soviet Leaders is an especially revealing work both because of its sweeping indictment of modern society and because it initiated a still-continuing debate within the dissident community. Originally drafted in 1973 as a set of reform proposals for the eyes of top Soviet leaders, it was subsequently released for publication only after the author was convinced that no official response was forthcoming. In it, Solzhenitsyn offers a scathing critique of Western culture and technological progress—he sees Soviet Marxism as merely an especially pernicious variation of the general Western drive for industrialization and modernization —and outlines some positive recommendations to return Russia to a distinctly non-Western pattern of development. His basic arguments are subsequently further elaborated and refined in later works such as *From Under the Rubble* and *Warning to the West*. For the sake of order, his comments can be divided into three subject areas: (1) attitudes toward political and social legitimacy, (2) views on social and political change, and (3) comments on the nature of an ideal future society.

POLITICAL AND SOCIAL LEGITIMACY

The key to understanding Solzhenitsyn's concept of political and social legitimacy—that is, the basis on which the possession of social and political power may be justified—lies in his rejection of the rational-scientific world view which underlies modern industrial society, and his preference for a traditional, morally based social order held together by uniquely Russian historical, cultural, and ethnic ties. His basic premise is that modern industrial society has finally worked its way into a material, psychological, and moral cul-de-sac from which no escape is to be found in the optimistic assumption that man can rationally plan the material and social aspects of his environment. The result, as Solzhenitsyn sweepingly puts it in his *Letter to the Soviet Leaders*, is a "historical, psychological, and moral crisis affecting the entire culture and world outlook which were conceived at the time of the Renaissance and attained the peak of their expression with the eighteenth-century Enlightenment."⁴ For both tsarist and Soviet Russia, attempts to follow this example have meant borrowing both Western technology and an interlocking set of attitudes glorifying rationalism, industrialization, and a poorly defined notion of "progress." These, in turn, have fostered anthropocentric and manipulatory attitudes toward mankind, society, and the physical universe and have cut man off from his cultural and ethnic roots. While both modern Russia and the Western industrial states share the same "multiple impasse," Solzhenitsyn holds that the USSR is now in a paradoxical position. On the one hand, the impact of modernization has been less thoroughgoing in the Soviet Union; despite the obvious traumas of industrialization and collectivization, and the political impact of the Stalin years, Russia is still far behind the West (a perception of backwardness that Solzhenitsyn shares with Sakharov, although the former views it as providing a unique opportunity, while the latter holds it to be a source of national weakness). For Solzhenitsyn, this means that two or three decades yet remain to seek a way out of the impasse, although he is skeptical of both Western and Soviet leaders who "keep hoping for new scientific loopholes and inventions to stave off the day of retribution."⁵ But on the other hand, as presently constituted, the Soviet leadership is likely to be less flexible and inventive than its Western counterpart. As a consequence, continued slavish reliance on orthodox Marxism, which Solzhenitsyn views as merely another pernicious Western import poorly suited to the conditions of his homeland, will retard the emergence of an alternative world view. Under increasing pressure from intellectual dissidents, restive minority nationalities, and a wide spectrum of critics, Soviet leaders have shown a tendency to cling tenaciously to the tenets of Marxism-Leninism to justify their continued political dominance. To be sure, economic and managerial reforms have been attempted, albeit with mixed success, and measures have been taken to upgrade historically disadvantaged groups such as collective farmers. But in these cases, the thrust of the measures has been to rationalize the system through fine tuning the planning and managerial apparatus and to intensify party control over an increasingly complex and potentially disjointed society; those fundamental aspects of Marxism-Leninism that define the party's preeminent role and establish a materialistic and positivistic world

view remain unchallenged.[6] Moreover, limited instrumental reforms have gone hand in hand with the increased repression of
intellectual dissidents whose criticism reaches beyond the issues of
free speech and human rights and into the area of fundamental
social values.

In contrast, in 1973 Solzhenitsyn was initially optimistic about
Western thinkers who, free of a restrictive ideological heritage,
have begun to probe for new ways of understanding the material
and moral dimensions of advanced industrial societies. He was
especially impressed by the work of the Teilhard de Chardin
Society and the Club of Rome, both of which have questioned the
value of continued material "progress."[7] By 1976, however,
Solzhenitsyn had become more pessimistic, charging that "the
West is on the verge of a collapse created by its own hands."[8]
Speaking to an essentially Western audience through the BBC,
he sought to answer the charges of both pro-Western Soviet
dissidents and Western analysts that he had been unfairly critical
of the West by noting that "I am not a critic of the West. I am a
critic of the weakness of the West. I am a critic of a fact which
I can't comprehend: how one can lose one's *spiritual strength*."[9]
(Emphasis added.) Observing that the process of "moral regeneration" in the Soviet Union was proceeding more slowly than anticipated because of the effectiveness of repressive measures. Solzhenitsyn argued that the West should hold firmly to its spiritual
values or face imminent collapse.[10]

Solzhenitsyn's indictment of the West had further hardened by
the time of his Harvard commencement address in June, 1978.
Claiming to see the "telltale symptoms by which history gives
warning to a threatened or perishing society," he charged a loss
of "civic courage" and a "lack of manhood," especially among the
"ruling and intellectual elites."[11] He once again pointedly rejected
the West as a model for Russian society, noting "the weakening
of human personality in the West while in the East [that is in Russia
and Eastern Europe] it has become firmer and stronger" due to
the superior "spiritual training" imposed by suffering through
decades of communist rule.[12]

The Harvard address also marked a broadening of the intellectual
base of Solzhenitsyn's criticism of Western society.. Content in
earlier comments merely to indict the "rationalistic" or "techno-

logical" bent of Western thought since the Enlightenment, he now linked it to the rise of humanism which "made man the measure of all things on earth—imperfect man, who is never free of pride, self-interest, envy, vanity, and dozens of other defects."[13] Terming this "rationalistic humanism," Solzhenitsyn lamented the false liberation of mankind from any higher moral force and the "calamity of an autonomous, irreligious humanistic consciousness."[14]

For Solzhenitsyn, the rejection of a rational-scientific and humanistic view of society leads to the substitution of historical, cultural, and ethnic factors as the touchstones of political and social legitimacy. Unlike Western theory, in which legitimacy has been achieved through reference to a combination of representative institutions and the possession of property and relevant skills, Solzhenitsyn's concept of legitimacy is linked to the embodiment of a sense of unique national identity and purpose. Legitimacy comes not from a prescribed set of institutional procedures or from the possession of an esoteric truth dictated by an imported, Western ideology, but from an acting out of the nation's unique historical mission and cultural unity. Looking backward to the Slavophile movement of the prerevolutionary era which argued that Russia's unique economic conditions and traditions could permit it to avoid the worst excesses of industrialization, he condemns both the nineteenth-century Russian Westernizers, who argued that the only salvation lay in imitating the West, and the Marxists, who made their own special variation of the same argument:

They [both Westernizers and Marxists] hounded the men who said that is was perfectly feasible for a colossus like Russia, with all its spiritual peculiarities and folk traditions, to find its own particular path; and that it could not be that the whole of mankind should follow a single, absolutely identical pattern of development.[15]

The eventual victory of both the Westernizers and their Marxist successors resulted in a pattern of development which led the nation far down what Solzhenitsyn regards as a dead-end path:

No, we had to be dragged along the whole of the Western bourgeois-industrial and Marxist path in order to discover, toward the close of the twentieth century, and again from progressive Western scholars, what any village graybeard in the Ukraine or Russia had understood from time immemorial and could have explained to the progressive commentators ages ago, had the commentators ever found the time in that dizzy fever of theirs to consult him: that a dozen worms can't go on and on gnawing the same apple forever, that if the earth is a finite object, then its expanses and resources are finite also, and the endless, infinite progress dinned into our heads by the dreamers of the Enlightenment cannot be accomplished on it. No, we had to shuffle on and on behind other people, without knowing what lay ahead of us, until suddenly we now hear the scouts calling to one another: We've blundered into a blind alley, we'll have to turn back. All that "endless progress" turned out to be an insane, ill-considered, furious dash into a blind alley.[16]

Commenting on Sakharov's *Progress, Coexistence, and Intellectual Freedom*, which he had seen in draft form before it circulated in *samizdat* among other dissidents, Solzhenitsyn argues that the model of a "progressive," rational society which the scientist presents "come[s] close to our idea of hell on earth."[17] He grants Sakharov the benefit of the doubt, however, and concludes that the description of a future rationalized society was "not intended to read literally" and that the primary message was the "moral disquiet" of the father of the Russian hydrogen bomb who "did not burn his plans in time."[18]

At the root of Solzhenitsyn's views on what constitutes political and social legitimacy in the Russian context are two interrelated premises: (1) that Russian society is essentially organic, combining strains of historical experience, cultural isolation from the West, and an all-permeating sense of ethnic and religious identity which Solzhenitsyn would term simply Russian nationalism, and (2) that Russia not only can but must follow a separate path of economic and social development. Political legitimacy is thus conveyed to those elements of the society most conscious of this national uniqueness and purpose. It therefore follows that the artificial Western concept of ideology, and especially its pernicious manifestations in socialism and communism, must be rejected before a process of national regeneration can begin.

In Solzhenitsyn's view, ideology per se lies at the root of many of the ills of the twentieth century. As embodiments of mankind's attempts to reshape society, ideologies are antithetical to the organically inspired notions of ethnic and cultural self-identity which the author holds to be the true essence of nationalism. Rather than emerging from within the cultural milieu, they are imposed from abroad or by indigenous zealots out of touch with their own society and eager to thrust an artificial "social theory" on others. Ideology alone accounts for the single-minded determination and fanaticism of true believers who uproot traditional cultures and demand total, unswerving allegiance for the sake of building a new social order.[19] "The horror of ideology," Solzhenitsyn concludes, "is precisely in its soul twisting."[20]

Solzhenitsyn sharply disagrees with Sakharov on the question or whether communist ideology is still a major driving force motivating the present Soviet leadership. To Sakharov, ideology has survived only as a meaningless facade and rationalization of the existing social order, while for Solzhenitsyn, communist ideology remains the "fetid root of present-day Soviet life" and an important influence on the day-to-day conduct of public affairs. The Soviet leaders are themselves "slaves of the Ideology," which is invested with a "mystical meaning" and regarded as a "deified truth." The tenacious attachment to ideology also "accounts for the rapt enchantment of the West for half a century" and its seeming tolerance of the regime in the name of social experimentation.[21]

While he rejects *all* ideologies as manifestations of a false consciousness, Solzhenitsyn predictably reserves his most vehement criticism for the doctrines of socialism and communism, which he regards as interchangeable variations on a common evil theme. He indicts socialism whole cloth as a doctrine that "of any type or shade leads to the total destruction of the human spirit and a leveling of mankind into death."[22] Solzhenitsyn rejects the notion that it is a perverted form of nineteenth-century humanism stripped of its religious content but still informed by a spirit of reformism.[23] Rather he relegates it to the status of a theory of "crude economic processes" devoid of "absolute concepts of morality."[24] In the place of any absolute morality stand both a highly relativistic definition of good and evil and a strong sense of tactical opportunism to seize upon moments of weakness on the part of anticommunist forces.[25]

Arguing that communism "is one and the same the whole world over," Solzhenitsyn refuses to accept the notion that individual national differences have molded the emergence of communist nations; rather the doctrine is held to be intrinsically "inimical to the national welfare, invariably striving to destroy the national organism in which it is developing."[26]

Solzhenitsyn also rejects the arguments that the Stalinist era was a perversion of a healthier Leninist system or that there have been any important internal changes within the Soviet Union since the *Vozhd*'s death. The murderous excesses of the Stalin years are read instead as the inevitable result of his emergence as "an heir to the spirit of Lenin's teaching," which counseled unprincipled opportunism and the suppression of opponents.[27] The present leadership fares little better; cast from the same Leninist-Stalinist mold, they are inherently incapable of setting aside their ideological blinders and comprehending the cultural and religious roots of the Russian nation. Even their sense of Soviet nationalism is an artless perversion of the true Russian national character. Instead of providing a healing and guiding presence by which the nation might be led to a reconciliation with its own past, it stresses instead xenophobic and aggressive features that have reinforced communism's own world-wide strategy.[28]

Solzhenitsyn is highly critical of those leaders and scholars in the West who are unconcerned with what he perceives as the threat of communist expansion and who are unaware of the seductive dangers of détente. Soviet communism is viewed as a doctrine "capable only of voracious expansion" even during a period marked by the "charade of détente."[29] "Communism will never desist," Solzhenitsyn tells us, "from its efforts to seize the world, be it through direct military conquest, through subversion and terrorism, or by subtly undermining society from within."[30] The short-term threat is immediate and real—he sees "an imminent danger of takeover in Western Europe and in many other parts of the world"[31]—and in the long run, Solzhenitsyn envisions apocalyptic struggle for world domination:

But in the case of communism, there is nothing to hope for: no reconciliation with communist doctrine is possible. The alternatives are either its complete triumph through the world or else its total collapse everywhere. The only salvation for Russia, for China, and for the entire world lies in the renunciation of this doctrine. Otherwise the world will face inexorable ruin.[32]

Shifting back to the domestic scene in his *Letter to the Soviet Leaders*, Solzhenitsyn appeals to what he hopes is a surviving sense of national identity among top Kremlin leaders to urge a return to traditional values and a rejection of Marxism-Leninism:

I am writing this letter on the supposition that you, too, are swayed by this primary concern [the survival of the Russian and Ukrainian people as the primary carriers of this cultural tradition], that you are not alien to your origins, to your fathers, grandfathers, and great grandfathers, to the expanses of your homeland; that you are conscious of your nationality.[33]

Marxism-Leninism is to be replaced by a sense of a moral regeneration based on traditional cultural and national values (although Solzhenitsyn does permit freedom of conscience) and a restructuring of the social order based on the assertion of a separate and vaguely chauvinistic pattern of national development. In the former instance, Solzhenitsyn urges "the inner, the moral, the healthy development of the people" to fill the psychological and moral void of a people nearly stripped of their cultural and national identity. He argues that only Christianity can provide the necessary sense of moral unity and purpose, although he does allow for the peaceful competition of conflicting views, including even Marxism as a political philosophy once it is stripped of the protective machinery of party and state.[34]

The unique path of national development envisioned by Solzhenitsyn is itself a combination of moral regeneration and national self-awareness. The key to this separate path lies in the renunciation of the "gigantic scale of modern technology" which has dominated both Western and Soviet thinking. In its place is to be built what the West has come to call a "zero-growth" or "steady state" economy centered on the development of the vast tracts of the Russian Northeast through modern but small-scale technology and the creation of small, environmentally integrated, and distinctly Russian cities to replace the chaotic sprawl of Russia's European urban centers.

There is also clearly a moral and value-creating purpose behind these proposals. When Solzhenitsyn speaks of "building anew" in the vast Northeast, he has in mind not only the creation of a small-scale and environmentally sound economy, but also the moral and psychological regeneration inherent in escaping the alienation of the cities and rebuilding a more traditional social and cultural order. The new industries and cities of the Northeast are to foster a cultural reawakening in which man is to be in harmony not only with technology and the environment, but also with his own religious, cultural, and national past.[35] These sentiments are further echoed in Solzhenitsyn's comments on the Northeast in *From Under in Rubble*. Arguing that the prospect of building anew in the Northeast "is like the wind in our faces," he again stresses the regenerative nature of such resettlement:

A family which has suffered a great misfortune or disgrace tries to withdraw into itself for a time to get over its grief by itself. This is what the Russian people must do: spend most of its time alone with itself, without neighbors or guests. It must concentrate on its *inner tasks: on healing its soul, educating its children, putting its own house in order.*

The healing of our souls! Nothing now is more important to us after all that we have lived through.[36] (Emphasis added.)

Such withdrawal and "repentance," as Solzhenitsyn terms it, will not only create a new social and economic order based on the principle of "self-limitation," but also set the stage for an eventual return of Russia to a role in world affairs to "set the whole world an example."[37]

There is also a chauvinistic ring to Solzhenitsyn's plan to develop the Northeast and to assert it as a distinctly Russian oasis in the modern world. In practical terms, he is clearly asking the nation to turn inward, not only in the sense of forsaking the ideologically motivated role of fostering world revolution or "fantastic alien global missions" (he sees Soviet backing of revolutionary movements and of existing communist regimes as a mistake and drain on national resources) and its world role as one of the military and economic superpowers, but also in the sense of limiting domestic goals for the sake of preserving the Russian homeland.[38] The nation's rich storehouse of mineral resources is to be carefully husbanded for future domestic consumption, and relations with other nations are to be limited to the minimum level necessary to maintain friendly ties.[39] The ideologically motivated cold war with China is to be ended, in part because of the new attention to domestic priorities and in part because the renunciation of official Marxism-Leninism would remove much of its rationale. But Solzhenitsyn refuses to yield on the question of Chinese territorial claims in Siberia; while he acknowledges that a "historical sin" was committed in the sixteenth century, he concludes that "there is nothing whatsoever we can do now to rectify that."[40]

There is also clearly a trace of a Russian sense of manifest destiny in Solzhenitsyn's comments on the impact of Soviet development on the Northeast's non-Russian peoples:

According to the census, the people of the North number 128,000 in all, thinly scattered and strung out across vast distances. We would not be crowding them in the slightest by opening up the North. Quite the contrary, *we are now sustaining their way of life and their existence as a matter of course; they seek no separate destiny for themselves and would be unable to find one.*[41] (Emphasis added.)

The argument is repeated in *From Under the Rubble*, although the author admits that his "heart sinks at the thought of our age-old sin in oppressing and destroying the indigenous peoples." But since there is only a "faint sprinkling" of native peoples in the Northeast, Solzhenitsyn paternalistically concludes that "it is permissible for us to seek our future there, so long as we show a tender fraternal concern for the natives, help them with their daily lives, educate them, and do not forcibly impose our ways on them."[42]

These touches of Russian manifest destiny are further justified, in Solzhenitsyn's view, by "the incomparable sufferings of our people."[43] He is unambiguous in asserting their deserving nature: "I would not consider it moral to recommend a policy of saving only ourselves, when the difficulties are universal, had our people not suffered more in the twentieth century, as I believe they have, than any other people in the world."[44] Citing the loss of one-third of the nation's potential population and almost one-half of its material wealth in two world wars, revolution and civil war, and internal political strife, Solzhenitsyn concludes that "we may permit ourself a little luxury, in the way an invalid is given a rest after a serious illness."[45]

The ultimate fate of the Ukraine evokes a far more tolerant attitude from Solzhenitsyn. He acknowledges that it is a "painful problem" because of centuries of unfeeling Russian domination and urges his fellow Russians to "show sense" in permitting the Ukrainians to make their own decision concerning federation or separation. But his own preferences clearly lie with continued close association, and he voices the hope that a tolerant and understanding attitude at this time will make it easier for the Ukrainians themselves to recognize that "not all problems are solved by secession."[46]

Solzhenitsyn's attitude toward Jews living in the Soviet Union is ambivalent. On the one hand, he clearly acknowledges that they have been singled out both by the tsarist order and the Soviet regime for special repressive measures. The excesses of the Black Hundreds are readily acknowledged, as is Stalin's special hatred of them, manifested in the destruction of the Zionist Socialist Party and its Jewish communes in the Crimea in the 1920s, the ominous implication of Jews in the Doctors' Plot that preceded the *Vozhd*'s death, and his malevolent selection of the desolate Birobidzhan province as the Jewish autonomous region.[47]

Solzhenitsyn also joins in celebrating the historic preservation of a unique Jewish culture, true to its religion and traditions. In *From Under the Rubble*, he lauds the "miraculous birth and consolidation of Israel after two thousand years of dispersal" as proof that an oppressed culture can survive seemingly total suppression, only to emerge intact and revitalized from the souls of those few who had never compromised identity and faith. Solzhenitsyn has clearly described the ultimate rebirth of the "true" Russian nation in much the same vein, and there is an unmistakable tone of admiration and respect in his attitude toward the emergence of a Jewish national homeland.[48]

It is more difficult to discern Solzhenitsyn's attitude toward the

role of Jewish dissidents in the Soviet Union itself and their ultimate fate in the sort of Russia that the writer would will upon the
nation. One thing is clear, however; at no time does Solzhenitsyn
venture close to the traditional themes of Russian anti-Semitism.
The condescension evident in his writings about the Ukrainians
is absent from his response to the growing role of the Jewish
minority in the dissident movement. Taking Solzhenitsyn at his
word that the new order would guarantee both religious freedom
and civil liberties, one must conclude that Jews remaining within
Russia would be permitted both to preserve their own unique
identity and to play an active role in the public deliberation of the
course of the nation, subject only to the restriction binding on all
that they not resort to the formation of cliques and parties or place
the interests of one group before the nation as a whole. No less
than any other nationality or minority, they would be accorded
their own special identity and given the opportunity to take part
in the sort of unstructured public discussion that Solzhenitsyn
envisions as the political process of the new Russia. To be sure,
they would clearly remain a minority within the nation as a whole;
while Solzhenitsyn's sense of cultural pluralism affords them both
identity and freedom, it does not countenance the notion of minority
veto. As must all other members of the community, Jews are expected to be governed by a conscious sense of self-restraint.

On two other issues, however, Solzhenitsyn is highly critical
both of Jewish dissidents within the USSR and of their Western
supporters. In the first instance, he is genuinely offended that both
domestic and foreign critics equate his call for a resuscitation of
Russian nationalism with the inevitable revitalization of traditional
anti-Semitic themes. Just as his "true" Russian nationalism is antithetical to the Western ideology of communism, so too does it
stand in clear contrast with the perversions wrought by tsarist and
Soviet officials as well, who have played upon anti-Semitic
themes for political gain.[49] The criticism of Andrei Sakharov that
the moderate theorists of benevolent ethnic and cultural nationalism are the precursors of a subsequent generation of chauvinistic
and aggressive nationalists is rejected out of hand, as is the commentary of emigré analysts such as Alexander Yanov, who argues
that any resuscitation of Russian nationalism will be exploited by

the Soviet regime itself to displace the blame for its own lack-luster performance on convenient scapegoats within the USSR.[50]

Solzhenitsyn is also highly critical of Jewish dissidents within the USSR for placing primary emphasis on the right of emigration rather than the more central question of political oppression per se. With the singular determination of a prophet who insists that the battle for the fate of Russia must be joined by all who oppose the current order, Solzhenitsyn predictably is disturbed by any forces that, in his view, attempt to redefine the central issue of the internal transformation of Russia to the "warped view that the main problem in the USSR today is that of emigration."[51] For this reason, Sakharov's long-standing endorsement of Jewish emigration has continually drawn fire from Solzhenitsyn as a distortion of priorities. Yet as William Korey, American director of the B'nai B'rith United Nations Office and an insightful commentator on the dissident movement, has observed, it was not until the mid 1970s— that is, after Solzhenitsyn's exile—that Jewish dissidents themselves began to recognize the need to form alliances with other internal critics and to spread the basis of their opposition from the narrow issue of emigration to larger questions of democratic reform.[52]

In spite of his reservations that concern with emigration charts a false course, Solzhenitsyn has concluded more recently in exile that a nation's right to self-identity supercedes any short-term political considerations: "Does it follow that we are entitled to advise Jews to forego the quest for their spiritual and national origins? Of course not. Are we all not entitled to live our natural life on the earth and to strive toward our individual goals, without heed for what others may think . . . ?"[53]

Several years after his initial comments in *Letter to the Soviet Leaders* and under fire from Sakharov and others who accused him of Great Russian chauvinism, Solzhenitsyn returned to the themes of Russian nationalism and the special suffering of his nation. Reminding his critics that he had argued in his Nobel lecture that "Nations are the wealth of mankind, its generalized personalities. The least among them has its own special colors and harbors within itself a special facet of God's design," he lamented that

. . . as soon as I drew the conclusion that it applies to the Russian people *too*, that the Russian people *also* have a right to national consciousness, to a national rebirth in the wake of the most excruciating spiritual illness, this was furiously labeled great power nationalism. . . . Russians are not supposed to be able to love their own people without hating others. We Russians are forbidden to breathe a word not only about national rebirth, but even about "national consciousness."[54]

Responding also to Sakharov's charge that he had exaggerated the suffering of the Russian and Ukrainian peoples, Solzhenitsyn pointed out that the civil war and the early phases of Stalinist terror took their greatest toll among those two nationalities, with the blows which fell on the peoples of Central Asia, the Caucasus, and eventually the Baltic states delayed until the central homeland had been secured.[55]

Content with defending his interpretation of Russian nationalism as a positive and value-creating force for the moral and spiritual regeneration of his people, Solzhenitsyn turns his attention to describing the legitimate "carriers" of these views in modern Soviet society. Rejecting the notion expressed by Sakharov and others in the scientific intelligentsia that in modern society one must look to the technocratic elite to generate new moral and spiritual values, he argues that only the literary intelligentsia can express the cumulative spirit of a nation:

In our own countries, torn by differences among parties, movements, castes, and groups, who for ages past has been not the dividing but the uniting force? *This, essentially, is the position of writers, spokesmen of a national language, of the chief tie binding the nation*, the very soil which the people inhabit, and *in fortunate circumstances, the nation's spirit too*.[56] (Emphasis added.)

While he maintains the argument that the role of the literary intelligentsia is to be collective spokesman of the national culture and the cornerstone of reigniting a sense of national identity, Solzhenitsyn is far less clear concerning the exact political function of this chosen strata. On the one hand, he personally rejects the role of the leader of the political opposition. In a contentious discussion before the Secretariat of the Board of the Soviet Writers' Union in 1967, he termed "sickening" the charge that the West viewed him as a leader of a political movement, rhetorically adding: "A creative writer and a leader of the political opposition. How do they fit together?"[57] But on the other hand, he has never underestimated the political *significance*, if not the direct political role, of a major literary figure in opposition to the regime. Speaking through a character in *The First Circle*, he elevates the critical function of such literary figures to the level of a "second government": "After all, the writer is a teacher of the people; surely that's what we've always understood? And a great writer—forgive me, perhaps I shouldn't say this, I'll lower my voice—a great writer is, so to speak, a second government."[58]

Intent on making his point that this sense of national spirit is embodied in only a handful of individuals at present, Solzhenitsyn further limits his definition of the "carriers" of this new national self-awareness to a "narrow circle" of writers and other members of the humanities-oriented intelligentsia who are "capable of independently rediscovering cultural treasures and values."[59] Referring to the new Soviet intelligentsia as merely "smatterers" who comprise the nation's "semi-educated estate" of rulers and apologists, he asserts that "we are different."[60] So different, in fact, that Solzhenitsyn recommends that the entire concept of the intelligentsia be scrapped as inappropriate for the "carriers" of national and cultural values. He predicts that they will come to be known in a more spiritual vein as simply "the righteous," who will constitute, at least until their numbers grow, a "sacrificial elite" whose moral purity will eventually transform the nation.[61] Within this setting, Solzhenitsyn clearly sees himself and his literary work as major contributors to defining the new sense of morality and national spirit, although it would be unfair to suggest that he claims all the limelight. Rather he envisions a process in which his "righteous" intelligentsia will enlarge as a consequence of the continuing efforts of dissidents to reawaken Russia to traditional moral and cultural values and the increasing willingness of disaffected citizens to engage in a form of intellectual passive resistance to avoid "living the lie," as Solzhenitsyn puts it.

Solzhenitsyn acknowledges that his "righteous" intelligentsia will initially face hardships and opposition, not only from official circles seeking to perpetuate the *status quo,* but also more insidiously from within the dissident community itself in the form of opposition to his concepts of nationalism and morality. Noting that the intelligentsia and "progressive society" of prerevolutionary Russia soundly condemned now venerated literary figures for their "reactionary" views, Solzhenitsyn offers candid insight into his own self-image:

What people prized in *Gogol* was his denunciation of the state system and the ruling classes. *But the moment he embarked upon the spiritual quest that was dearest of all to him he was flayed by the journalistic press and excommunicated from progressive society.* Tolstoy was prized for the same sort of denunciations and also for his animosity toward the Church and toward higher philosophy and creation. *But his insistent moralizing, his summons to the simple life, to nonresistance to evil and to universal goodness met with a condescending reception.* The "reactionary" Dostoyevsky was altogether detested by the intelligentsia. *He would have been trampled underfoot and forgotten in Russia . . . had he not suddenly surfaced in the twentieth century to thunderous worldwide fame in the respected West.*[62] (Emphasis added.)

But while this "nucleus of an intelligentsia," in which Solzhenitsyn sees "our hope for spiritual renewal," is to serve as the active creator and "carrier" of a renewed sense of benevolent and moralistic nationalism, a no less important role is reserved for the common man, who is seen as the passive repository of traditional values. Solzhenitsyn's argument that the people have retained an inherent sense of morality and national self-consciousness that can be reawakened by the "righteous" intelligentsia is based on the assumption that the population manifests only a *pro forma* acceptance of the official order and has privately retreated into a pattern of spiritual and intellectual noninvolvement. In a rambling passage in *From Under the Rubble,* Solzhenitsyn asserts that the distinctive Russian *narod* survives and "takes no part in the official lie":

It is rashness to conclude that the people no longer exist. Yes, the village has been routed and its remnants choked, yes, the outlying suburbs are filled with the click of dominoes (one of the achievements of universal literacy) and broken bottles, there are no traditional costumes and no folk dances, the language has been corrupted and thoughts and ambitions even more deformed and misdirected; but why is it that not even these broken bottles, nor the litter blown back and forth by the wind in city courtyards, fills one with such despair as the careerist hypocrisy of the smatterers? It is because *the people* on the whole *take no part in the official lie,* and this today is its most distinctive feature, *allowing one to hope that it is not,* as its accusers would have it, *utterly devoid of God.* Or at any rate, *it has preserved a spot in its heart that has still not been scorched or trampled to death.*[63] (Final emphasis added.)

But if not "trampled to death," who then are the illusive *narod,* and what uncorrupted truths and values lie below their stoic endurance of the present order? On these issues, Solzhenitsyn offers no clear answers. While he detests the impact of urbanization and "massovization" of traditional Russian culture, Solzhenitsyn resists the temptation to equate the surviving vestiges of traditional society solely with the peasantry. Perhaps the closest he comes to the creation of such a peasant ikon lies in the sympathetic treatment accorded to Matryona in *Matryona's House* or to the janitor Spiridon in *The First Circle.* Yet Matryona, an aging peasant teasing out a marginal existence outside of the collective farm, is offered more as an embodiment of stoic human endurance, as her world—and literally her home—are malevolently disassembled by parasitic relatives, than as a positive character manifesting any purposive or coherent concept of the illusive Russian essence. Solzhenitsyn offers her simply as "that one righteous person without whom, as the saying goes, no city can stand. . . . Neither can the whole world."[64]

Spiridon, on the other hand, is seemingly offered as a more coherent embodiment of "homespun truth" and is befriended in the *sharashka* (a research institute staffed by qualified prisoners) by Gleb Nerzhin, the Solzhenitsyn surrogate, who seeks to complete his own metamorphosis from former member of the Soviet intelligentsia to man of the "people." But the path doubles back on reality. When first "tossed down among the people," Nerzhin sought wisdom in the simplicity of their lives:

He strove for simplicity, to rid himself of the intelligentsia's habits of extreme politeness and intellectual extravagance. In a time of hopeless failure, amid the wreckage of his shattered life, Nerzhin believed that the only people who mattered were those who planed wood, worked metal, plowed land, and cast iron with their own hands. He tried to acquire from simple working people the wisdom of capable hands and their philosophy of life. And so he came full circle back to the fashion of the previous century: the creed that one must "go to the people."[65]

And yet in the "harsh apprenticeship of the camps, one more of Nerzhin's illusions disappeared." The common people lacked the "homespun superiority" that had allegedly sustained them and intrigued Nerzhin—they suffered as deeply, doubted as profoundly, and connived and betrayed as perversely as anyone else for the favor of camp warders or for the tiniest scrap of food. What they lacked, Nerzhin concluded, was "a point of view"—something created in the milieu of language and culture but informed and given structure by the "inner self" through a continuing moral dialectic within the soul. Thus formed Nerzhin's new understanding of the meaning of the "people":

Having got over one more bout of enthusiasm, Nerzhin . . . understood the people in a new way, a way he had not read about anywhere: the people is not everyone who speaks our language, nor yet the elect marked by the fiery stamp of genius. Not by birth, not by the work of one's hands, not by the wings of education is one elected into the people.

But by one's inner self.

Everyone forges his inner self year after year.

One must try to temper, to cut, to polish one's soul so as to become a *human being*.

And thereby become a tiny particle of one's own people.[66] (Emphasis in original.)

SOCIAL AND POLITICAL CHANGE

Having asserted that the core of the "righteous" intelligentsia is composed of a growing band of individuals (not necessarily scholars or intellectuals) who are capable of recognizing and embodying the nation's unique cultural heritage, Solzhenitsyn is anxious to deny that the processes of economic modernization and social change since the revolution have created a new technological and managerial elite that is the legitimate inheritor of social and political power. It must be understood that Solzhenitsyn is not arguing that individual scientists or members of the technocratic elite cannot emerge as important dissident figures and play a role in destroying both the passivity of their colleagues and the official veil of repression and deception; quite to the contrary, he frequently lauds the personal courage and political significance of Andrei D. Sakharov and other dissident scientists. But he does dispute their contention that the rational-technical world view which underlies their approach to positive reforms is an important value-creating force and that these groups, as identifiable social elements, can have any positive, meaningful impact in building a new social order. At the root of this rejection is Solzhenitsyn's assumption that the most important need of the nation is not political reform or the modernization of an overly bureaucratized, conservative elite, but a regeneration of moral and spiritual values. Thus he challenges Sakharov's argument that the technical intelligentsia will also serve not only as the carriers of political and social rationality, but also as the carriers of humanistic values more in tune with the Western notions of the worth and dignity of the individual. Noting that Sakharov vaguely envisions rule by an "intellectual elite," Solzhenitsyn points out that "he *instinctively* expects it to be a moral elite," an optimism that Solzhenitsyn does not share.[67]

Much of the political weakness of the scientific intelligentsia stems, in Solzhenitsyn's view, from their narrow-minded concern with the creation of physical culture and their tendency to feel themselves superior to those elements of the intellectual community concerned with the arts and culture. Expressing his contempt for Soviet scientists who keep their thoughts "at the level of their test tubes,"[68] Solzhenitsyn speaks of their de facto implication in the offenses of the regime:

In the warm, well-lit, well-equipped rooms of their research institutes, the "pure" scientists and technicians, while roundly condemning their brothers in the arts for "toadying to the regime," have become accustomed to overlooking their own innocuous service to the state; but that service is no less terrible, and history will make them answer no less harshly for it.[69]

Solzhenitsyn's indictment also includes the worldwide scientific community, which has timorously resisted both the moral and political roles which their command of modern science might have permitted them to play:

One might have thought that the structure of the modern world would be entirely in the hands of scientists, since it is they who decide all the technical steps of mankind. One might have thought that the direction in which the world is to move would be determined by a worldwide concord of scientists, not of politicians. . . . But no, scientists have made no explicit attempts to become an important independently motivated force within mankind. Entire congresses of them back away from the suffering of others: it is cozier to remain within the limits of science. The same spirit of Munich has spread its enervating wings over them.[70]

Solzhenitsyn reserves his most strident criticism for those in the technical intelligentsia—he terms them "smatterers," like the apologists for the regime, although they seek reform—who reject their national culture in condescending terms:

In 1969 this surge of self-satisfaction on the part of the scientific and technical smatterers spilled out into *samizdat* with an article by Semyon Telegin (pseudonymous, of course), entitled "What Is to Be Done?" The tone is that of a breezy, pushing know-it-all, quick at side associations and with a familiar, low wit . . . , at one moment *showing his contempt for the population with which*

he is obliged to share the same plot of dry land ("the human pigsty"),
at another indulging in rhetorical flourishes.[71] (Emphasis added.)

Condemning Telegin for placing his faith in "a class of highly
educated people *armed with the ideas of modern science,* able,
independent, fearless thinkers, altogether accustomed to think
and fond of thinking, *but not plowing the land,*" Solzhenitsyn
rejects the notion that it is possible "to apply the methodology of
physics to the subtleties of ethics."[72] Telegin's argument that the
scientific intelligentsia's proper reformist role is to generate a counter-
culture through their passive resistance and intellectual independence
and then to "act as yeast" in terms of "inculcating into the people
an understanding of what we ourselves have come to understand"
as "skilled missionaries of the new culture" is rejected out of hand
by Solzhenitsyn. While he agrees that "secret conspiracies and new
parties" would be inappropriate, he argues that more than the
author's intellectual arrogance and "nonacceptance of the oppressors' culture" will be required to awaken the Russian people
to the need for "spiritual power."[73]

Solzhenitsyn also denies that a separate and politically significant managerial intelligentsia has arisen as a consequence of
modernization. While he acknowledges that in the 1950s, and even
more so in the 1960s, "leading members of the intelligentsia . . .
were increasingly allowed to occupy high-level posts as the technological requirements for all forms of management grew," he rejects the contention, held both by Soviet dissidents like Sakharov
and by some Western commentators on Soviet affairs, that a
technocracy has developed:

There also exists the following theory: that now, *thanks to the*
growth of technology, there is a technocracy in the Soviet Union,
a growing number of engineers, and the engineers are now running
the economy and they, not the party, will soon determine the fate
of the country. *But I will tell you that the engineers will determine*
the fate of the country just as much as our generals will determine
the fate of the army. That means zero. Everything is done the way
the party demands.[74] (Emphasis added.)

When speaking of his own preferences for domestic political change, Solzhenitsyn returns to the concept of an organic society sustained through a renewed sense of its national and cultural heritage. Since it is from its integrated historical and cultural roots that the nation derives its special identity and sense of mission, any change that might abruptly break with that tradition or hand over power to narrow, self-serving interests must be resisted. Thus Solzhenitsyn opposes revolutionary change of the present authoritarian system and the creation of a pluralist democratic state in which the competition of organized political groups would allegedly lose sight of the organic unity of the nation. Rather he foresees the continuance of an authoritarian political order, but one converted to the expression of Russia's unique sense of historical and cultural purpose. While he provides for the free competition of political philosophies (but not of organized political groups) and the resuscitation of the soviets as representative institutions, it is clear that he favors the emergence of a stable, traditional authoritarian system which embodies his sense of the traditional moral order which sets Russia apart from the West.

Solzhenitsyn rejects the notion of revolutionary political change both for his native land and for other nations:

. . . I have become an opponent of all revolutions and all armed convulsions, including future ones. . . . Intensive study has convinced me that bloody mass revolutions are always disastrous for the people in whose midst they occur. And in our present-day society I am by no means alone in that conviction. The sudden upheaval of any hastily carried-out change of the present leadership (the whole pyramid) might provide only a new and destructive struggle and would certainly lead to only a very dubious gain in the quality of leadership.[75]

Solzhenitsyn is also certainly not enamored of Western democratic institutions. Referring to it as "democracy run riot," he indicts the freewheeling style of electoral campaigns in which politicians make sweeping promises to gain support. At the root of this riotous democracy are both the seemingly limitless demands of citizens, groups, and special interests and the abject failure of the state to control and coordinate their activities because of its legalistic approach to political life:

Every conflict is solved according to the letter of the law and this is considered to be the ultimate solution. If one is right from a legal point of view, nothing more is required, nobody may mention that one could still not be entirely right, and urge self-restraint or a renunciation of these rights, call for sacrifice and selfless risk. . . . Voluntary self-restraint is almost unheard of: everybody strives toward further expansion to the extreme limit of legal frames.[76]

Noting that a lawless society is equally objectionable, Solzhenitsyn still concludes that whenever "the tissue of life is woven of legalistic relationships, this creates an atmosphere of spiritual mediocrity that paralyzes man's noblest impulses."[77]

Solzhenitsyn's strongest criticism is directed, however, at the notion of organized political competition among self-serving interests which collectively do not represent the organic will of the nation. Initially taking up the point in his *Letter to the Soviet Leaders*, he argues that democracies per se may fall victim to "misdirection":

While even in an established democracy we can see many instances when a fatal course of action is chosen as a result of self-deception, or of a random majority caused by the swing of a small and unpopular party between two big ones—and it is this insignificant swing, which in no way expresses the will of the majority (and even the will of the majority is not immune to misdirection), which decides vitally important questions in national and sometimes even world politics. And there are very many instances today of groups of workers who have learned to grab as much as they can for themselves whenever their country is going through a crisis, even if they ruin the country in the process.[78]

Such a democracy is particularly ill suited to contemporary Russia because of her lack of experience with representative institutions. Solzhenitsyn notes that "for sheer lack of practice," the

democratic institutions created after the February revolution survived for only eight months. Recent experience has only lessened
the likelihood that a multiparty democracy could now succeed
where it had once failed, leading Solzhenitsyn to conclude that
any attempts to create such a system would "merely be a melancholy
repetition of 1917."[79]

Having seen his views on political change become the object of
widespread criticism from some dissident circles and from Western
commentators, Solzhenitsyn has frequently returned to the themes
of democracy and political pluralism in subsequent publications.
Writing in 1975 to point out what he viewed as the most important
remaining theoretical differences between himself and Sakharov,
Solzhenitsyn once again rejected "the sudden advent . . . of total
democracy" [a considerable distortion of Sakharov's own views].
Arguing that he has been "falsely charged with having a total
aversion to democracy in general, instead of doubts about a sudden
introduction of democracy into the present-day U.S.S.R.," he
cites as justification of his continuing skepticism the "extreme
danger of wars between nationalities that will drown in the blood
of the birth of democracy, should it occur in the absence of strong
authority."[80] Moreover, he traces the development of contemporary
totalitarian regimes not from traditional authoritarian systems,
but from the "crisis of democracy, from the failure of irreligious
humanism."[81]

Solzhenitsyn also denies that a process of convergence is occurring
between the United States and the Soviet Union. A natural outgrowth of his rejection of the argument that technological change
in all advanced industrial nations leads to the emergence of similar
socioeconomic systems and pragmatic world views—the so-
called postindustrial society of Daniel Bell and others—Solzhenitsyn's
denial is linked both to his view that the technocratic intelligentsia
is not the legitimate heir of social and political power and to his
opposition to the emergence of a new "mass culture" which will
replace both traditional norms of social conduct and current
ideologies. He is especially critical of attempts within his nation
to create such a new "mass culture" at the expense of "the people,"
who, it should be recalled, are thought of as the passive carriers
of traditional culture and spirituality:

Indeed, how could *the people* have survived? It has been subjected to two processes both tending toward the same end and each lending impetus to the other. One is the universal process (which, if it had been postponed any longer in Russia, we might have escaped altogether) of what is fashionably known as *massovization* (an abominable word, but then the process is no better), a product of the new Western technology, the sickening growth of cities, and the general standardization of methods of information and education. The second is our own special Soviet process, designed to rub off the age-old face of Russia and rub on another, synthetic one.[82] (Emphasis in original.)

Noting Sakharov's call for the "positive" convergence of capitalist and socialist systems, Solzhenitsyn rebukes the physicist for confusing objective analysis of social developments with his own "moral yearnings." Indeed, he reverses the argument to assert that the likely result of any process of convergence might well be two equally repressive societies:

Similarly, Sakharov's hopes of convergence are not a well-grounded scientific theory, but *a moral yearning* to cloak man's last, nuclear, sin, to avoid nuclear catastrophe. (If we are concerned with solving mankind's moral problems, the prospect of convergence is a somewhat dismal one: if two societies, each afflicted with its own vices, gradually draw together and merge into one, *what will they produce? A society immoral in the warp and the woof.*)[83] (Emphasis added.)

Solzhenitsyn reiterated the same charges in his Harvard commencement address in 1978, labeling convergence as but a "soothing theory" which bore little correspondence to the real world, especially since it also entailed "acceptance of the other side's defects."[84]

Perhaps because of his concern for domestic political change, Solzhenitsyn has been particularly critical of Sakharov's attention to international questions and the domestic politics of other nations. In a passage that mixes his sense of morality with his fear that attention to the difficulties of others may "distort" the development of a clear understanding of the problems of his homeland, Solzhenitsyn warns against the temptation to focus on external political events and moralize about the alleged shortcomings of others:

We see a conspicuous fault in the fact that the article [Sakharov's *Progress, Coexistence, and Intellectual Freedom*] lavishes attention on the internal problems of *other* countries—Greece, Indonesia, Vietnam, the United States, and China—while the situation in the USSR is exhibited in the most benevolent light, or rather, indulgently underlit. . . . We have the moral right to make judgments on international problems and still more on the internal problems of other countries, only if we take cognizance of *our own* internal problems and do penance for our faults.[85] (Emphasis in original.)

Perhaps more important at the root of his rejection of the Western concept of democracy or the seductive notion of convergence is his fear of the loss of the guiding principle of *self-limitation*, which Solzhenitsyn sees as the natural outgrowth of a process of national "repentance" and the renewal of traditional values. Such "self-limitation" serves not only as the key to building a new society and economy based on principles of conservationism and environmentalism, but also as the touchstone of the new political order. It is this "self-limitation" that is to check the role of aggressive individualism and political self-interest and provide for the emergence of a true national consensus and common will. In its absence—and Solzhenitsyn argues that it will certainly be absent in any multiparty democratic state—the nation will be torn apart either by the shifting will of the majority or by the avarice of special interests.[86]

This overriding concern with defending the true interest of the nation against contending and self-serving interests also predictably has an impact on Solzhenitsyn's thinking about the emergence of a multiparty system in Russia. Arguing that his nation should "rise above Western conceptions to a loftier viewpoint," he reminds his readers that " 'Partia' means a *part*. Every party known to history has always defended the interests of this one *part* against—whom? Against the rest of the people. And in the struggle with other parties it disregards justice for its own advantage."[87] Solzhenitsyn presses his attack on the notion of a multiparty democracy by pointing out that

its dangerous, perhaps mortal defects have become more and more obvious in recent decades, when superpowers are rocked by *party struggles with no ethical basis;* when a tiny party can hold the balance between two big ones and over an extended period determine the fate of its own and even neighboring peoples; when unlimited freedom of discussion can wreck a country's resistance to some looming danger and lead to capitulation in wars not yet lost; when the historical democracies prove impotent, faced with a handful of sniveling terrorists. *The Western democracies today are in a state of political crisis and spiritual confusion.* Today, more than at any time in the past century, it ill becomes us to see our country's only way out in the Western parliamentary system.[88] (Emphasis added.)

For Solzhenitsyn, the preferable path lies somewhere between the alleged chaos of Western parliamentary regimes and the imposed tyranny of a totalitarian regime that embodies an imported ideology. The key to understanding his concept of the ideal political system for his homeland lies in his notions of individual freedom, political authority, and the nature of the political process.

On the question of individual freedom, Solzhenitsyn offers a concept of freedom that stresses obligation rather than license. Warning that "external, or social freedom" is but a medium for growth and maturation instead of the "object of our existence," Solzhenitsyn argues that there is a "miscalculation in the urgent pursuit of political freedom as the first and main thing: we should first have a clear idea of what to do with it."[89] Such "external freedom" can be "only a framework within which other and higher aims can be realized."[90]

Turning to the question of intellectual freedom and freedom of information, which Sakharov sees as the necessary preconditions for political reform and for bringing Russia into the mainstream of world scientific thought, Solzhenitsyn argues that the greatest liability imposed by limitations on the exchange of information across national borders is that the *"world is not allowed to be-*

come one spiritually."[91] (Emphasis added.) Concerning the long-range domestic implications of such intellectual freedom, Solzhenitsyn holds a much less sanguine view than Sakharov:

Certainly intellectual freedom in our country would immediately bring about a great transformation and help us to cleanse ourselves of many stains. . . . But if we gaze into the far, far future—let us consider the West. The West has supped more than its fill of every kind of freedom, including intellectual freedom. And has this saved it? We see it today crawling on hands and knees, its will paralyzed, uneasy about the future, spiritually racked and dejected. Unlimited external freedom in itself is quite inadequate to save us. Intellectual freedom is a very desirable gift, but, like any sort of freedom, a gift of conditional, not intrinsic, worth, only a means by which we can attain another and higher goal.[92] (Emphasis added.)

To Solzhenitsyn, then, the Western notion of freedom, which stresses the absence of restraints on external behavior, is far less important for the rebirth of Russia than his own more Hegelian conception which focuses on the dual facets of "inner freedom of will" and external "self-restriction." Of the former, Solzhenitsyn says that "inner freedom" is necessary for self-awareness of one's place in the traditional moral order; threatened on the one hand by official repression—although he maintains that we can "assert our inner freedom even in external conditions of unfreedom"—and on the other by the unrelenting din of a mind-dulling mass culture, it is this kind of freedom that is presently being exercised by the "righteous" intelligentsia seeking to rediscover the nation's true spirit and reawaken such awareness in the people. It is the freedom to search not for unlimited intellectual license but for the unique spiritual essence of the Russian people—that is, Solzhenitsyn's concept of nationalism—that constitutes the "higher goal."[93]

On the latter concept of external "self-restriction," Solzhenitsyn argues that external, social freedom "is very desirable for the sake of undistorted growth."[94] Such freedom "is moral," he continues, "but only if it keeps within certain bounds. . . . And order is not immoral if it means a calm and stable system."[95] Rather his idea of freedom entails a sense of discipline and sacrifice associated with his concept of spiritual obligation. "After the Western ideal of unlimited freedom, after the Marxist concept of freedom as acceptance of the yoke of necessity—here is the true Christian definition of freedom. Freedom is *self-restriction!* Restriction of the self for the sake of others."[96] (Emphasis in original.)

Solzhenitsyn sees sweeping consequences for his sense of freedom as moral obligation and "self-restriction" both in reorienting human consciousness and in fostering peaceful political and social change:

Once understood and adopted, this principle diverts us—as individuals . . . societies, and nations—from *outward* to *inward* development, thereby giving us greater spiritual depth.

The turn toward *inward* development, the triumph of inwardness over outwardness . . . will be a great turning point in the history of mankind. . . . There will be a complete change not only in the direction of our interests and activities but in the very nature of human beings (a change from spiritual dispersal to spiritual concentration), and a greater change still in the character of human societies. If in some places this is destined to be a revolutionary process, these revolutions will not be like earlier ones—physical, bloody and never beneficial—but will be *moral revolutions*, requiring both courage and sacrifice, though not cruelty.[97] (Emphasis in original.)

Such inward development will also have profound consequences in the "material sphere" and in relations among nations:

But in the material sphere too this change will have conspicuous results. The individual will not flog himself to death in his greed for bigger and bigger earnings, but will spend what he has economically, rationally and calmly. The state will not . . . use its strength— sometimes even with no particular end in view—simply on the principle that where something will give, one must exert pressure . . . —no, *among states too the moral rule for individuals will be adopted*—do not unto others as you would not have done unto you. . . . Only thus can a well-ordered life be created on our planet.[98] (Emphasis added.)

It is also important to understand Solzhenitsyn's concept of political authority, which is rooted in his acceptance of traditional moral authority as the touchstone of political life. Looking back on the nation's distant past, he reminds the readers of *Letter to the Soviet Leaders* that "for a thousand years Russia lived with an authoritarian order—and at the beginning of the twentieth century both the physical and spiritual health of her people were still intact."[99] What made this system both viable and legitimate was that the

authoritian order possessed *a strong moral foundation*, embryonic and rudimentary though it was—*not the ideology of universal violence, but Christian Orthodoxy*, the ancient, seven-centuries-old Orthodoxy of Sergei Radonezhsky and Nil Sorsky, before it was battered by Patriarch Nikon and bureaucratized by Peter the Great [that is, before the first impact of Western thought]. From the end of the Moscow period and throughout the whole of the Petersburg period, once this moral principle was perverted and weakened, the authoritarian order, despite the apparent external successes of the state, gradually went into a decline and eventually perished.[100] (Emphasis added.)

Again taking up this theme in *From Under the Rubble*, Solzhenitsyn argues that such systems can offer definite advantages, especially when compared with the prospect for internal discord associated with parliamentary democracies, although there are dangers which must be avoided. He notes that "providing certain limits are not exceeded, they can offer people a tolerable life, much as any democratic republic can."[101] But he cautions that

together with their virtues of *stability, continuity, immunity from political ague*, there are, needless to say, great dangers and defects in authoritarian systems of government: the danger of dishonest authorities, upheld by violence, the danger of arbitrary decisions and the difficulty of correcting them, the danger of sliding into tyranny. *But authoritarian regimes as such are not frightening—only those which are answerable to no one and nothing*. The autocrats of earlier, religious ages, though their power was ostensibly unlimited, felt themselves responsible before God and their own consciences. *The autocrats of our own time are dangerous precisely because it is difficult to find higher values which would bind them.* [102] (Emphasis added.)

For Solzhenitsyn, such values are to be found in the resuscitation of traditional culture—that is, the spiritual essence of the Russian nation—and in the sense of "self-limitation," which he sees as the guiding principle of both public and private life. What is objectionable about the present authoritarian system is not that "it is undemocratic, authoritarian, based on physical constraints—a man can live in such conditions without harm to his *spiritual essence*," but that "over and above its physical and economic constraints, *it demands of us total surrender of our souls, continuous and active participation in the general, conscious lie.*"[103] (Emphasis added.) It is this denial of "inner freedom" that prevents the realization of Solzhenitsyn's concepts of freedom-as-obligation and "self-restraint" and retards the recognition of traditional moral limitations on the exercise of political power.

Both because he seeks such a traditional moral order, and because "we have never been shown any realistic path of transition from our present system to a democratic republic,"[104] Solzhenitsyn concludes that "for the foreseeable future, perhaps, whether we like it or not, whether we intend it or not, Russia is nevertheless destined to have an authoritarian order."[105] Arguing that this would be "the most natural, the smoothest, and least painful path of development,"[106] he calls in the *Letter to the Soviet Leaders* for "an authoritarian order, but one founded not on inexhaustible 'class hatred' but on love of your fellow men—not of your immediate entourage but sincere love for your whole people."[107]

The issue of authoritarian rule surfaces once again in Solzhenitsyn's 1980 essay in *Foreign Affairs*. Noting Western criticism of his seeming advocacy of authoritarian systems, he argues that "the most I called for was the renunciation of communist ideology . . . so as to allow at least a little more breathing space for the national spirit."[108] He acknowledges that "the only path from the icy cliff of totalitarianism I could propose was the slow and smooth descent via an authoritarian system," but he reminds the reader that in his

Letter, he subsequently qualified such authoritarianism to include "love of one's fellow man" and a "firm basis in law that reflects the will of the people."[109] Above all, he adds, it would be "a calm and stable system" that did not "degenerate into arbitrariness and tyranny."[110]

On the long-range question of whether Russia would remain a benevolent authoritarian order or develop democratic institutions, Solzhenitsyn professes to have formed "no final opinion."[111] "I have never attempted to analyze the whole question in theoretical terms," he confesses, and predicts that the final answer "can only emerge through an organic development of accumulated national experience."[112] Having offered these qualifications in his own defense, Solzhenitsyn nonetheless repeats the usual litany of charges against capricious democratic institutions. In a revealing passage, he reminds the reader that the "traditional social concepts" of historic Russian culture focused on defining *truth* (*pravda* in Russian) as justice in the ultimate moral sense rather than in the juridical meaning employed in Western society. *Truth* and *justice* thus are identical and are the ultimate moral standard against which any form of government must be measured. *Odno slovo pravdy* ("one word of truth") outweighs the accumulated wisdom of man's contrived laws. Even more importantly, "the truth cannot be determined by voting, since the majority does not necessarily have any deeper insight into the truth." Thus truth is to be sought by "mutual persuasion" among the representatives of the "people," gathered into assemblies which Solzhenitsyn compares to the ancient *zemskie sabory*. While such truth is not "legally binding" in the strict definition of modern law, it is nonetheless "morally incontestable."[113] This once again brings Solzhenitsyn to his indictment of political factionalism. "From this perspective, the creation of *parties*, that is, segments or parts which fight for their *partial interests* at the expense of other segments of the people, seems an absurdity. (Indeed, this is less than worthy of mankind, or at least of mankind in its potential.)"[114] (Emphasis in original.)

Solzhenitsyn's conception of the traditional moral basis of politics and his thoughts on the proper "self-restriction" of individual and group will combine to produce an understanding of the political process far different from Western notions of competitive pluralism. In practical terms, he calls for both freedom

of expression (constrained only by self-limitation in the interest
of the common good) and the competition of political philosophies,
but with one carefully drawn reservation: "So that the country
and people do not suffocate, and so that they all have the chance
to develop and enrich us with ideas, allow competition on an equal
and honorable basis—*not for power, but for truth*—between all
ideological and moral currents, in particular between all religions."[115]
(Emphasis added.) Clearly the author sees no contradiction between
his earlier criticism of a factional multiparty system and an organized struggle for political power on the one hand, and his
acceptance of a free debate over the nature of "truth" on the
other. Unfortunately Solzhenitsyn is unclear on the actual nature
of the political process beyond this rejection of the struggle for
political power and party politics. But extrapolating from his
statements about the role of writers and intellectuals as the spokesmen of various philosophies and the value of traditional cultural
norms as the rallying point in defining one's place within the
political order, one must assume that he has in mind a relatively
unstructured political process which denies legitimacy to organized
political groups as spokesmen for special interests or a mediating
power broker (that is, our notions of the group basis of politics and
the majority-building function of political parties) and sanctions
instead a much looser set of associational arrangements built
around clearly articulated ideologies or schools of thought. For
himself, he sees "Christianity today as the only living spiritual
force capable of undertaking the spiritual healing of Russia," but
he requests no special political role for the church, which he thinks
of more as a source of spiritual and moral truth than as a separate
political force per se.[116]

Solzhenitsyn also offers no clear view of his understanding of
the political role of secular associations. At one point in the *Letter
to the Soviet Leaders*, he argues that the Communist Party may
remain as a separate organization of "like-minded confederates"
if it is willing to "relinquish its Ideology, renounce its unattainable
and irrelevant missions of world domination, *and instead fulfill
its national missions* and save us from war with China and from
technological disaster."[117] (Emphasis added.) Among Western
students of Solzhenitsyn's thought, confusion exists on his attitude
toward other secular or professional associations. Reasoning from

the statements of some of the characters in *August 1914*, John Dunlop argues that he envisions a "popular assembly based on the vocational rather than territorial principle" and compares him with the emigré philosopher Nikolai Berdyaev, who advocated the creation of a syndicalist corporate state made up of the representatives of professional, economic, and cultural associations.[118] But against this interpretation must be weighed Solzhenitsyn's comments in *From Under the Rubble* and the *Nobel Lecture* that, given a lack of restraint, "every trade union and every corporation strives by all possible means to win the most advantageous position,"[119] or that "every professional group, as soon as it finds a convenient moment to RIP OFF A PIECE, unearned or not, extra or not, immediately rips it off, let all of society come crashing down."[120] (Capitalization in original.) Probably the best interpretation that can be given is that Solzhenitsyn himself is unsure of—or has not gone on public record concerning—the nature of the political process he wishes to emerge, except that it embody the search for philosophical and spiritual truth rather than the clash of partisan, self-serving interests. The one seemingly paradoxical point that he has been clear on, however, is his desire to see the soviets reemerge as viable popular assemblies cleansed, of course, of dominance by the Communist Party and transformed instead into a forum for "consultation with the working people," a curious formulation if these are to be fully empowered legislative bodies.[121]

Perhaps much of Solzhenitsyn's reticence on the *institutional form* of government and the *nature of political participation* stems from his understandable preoccupation with the more immediate question of political strategy to initiate change within his now-distant homeland. Rejecting revolutionary change because it leads to a precipitous break with the past, criticizing incremental political and economic reformism because it does not deal with the essential questions of spirituality and national self-consciousness, and pointing out that "we have never been shown any realistic path of transition . . . to a democratic republic," Solzhenitsyn calls instead for a process of transformation which begins with the inward moral rebirth of the individual. In *From Under the Rubble*, he explains how he "envisions this rebirth: by traveling our path of repentance, self-limitation, and inner development."[122] In tactical terms, this change will begin as a matter of individual rebirth without any sweeping challenge to the system and without the need for organized activity on the part of dissidents:

But let us note that if the absolutely essential task is not political liberation, but the liberation of our souls from participation in the lie forced upon us, then it requires no physical, revolutionary, social, organizational measures, no meetings, strikes, trade unions— things fearful for us even to contemplate and from which we quite naturally allow circumstances to dissuade us. No! It requires from each individual a moral step within his power—*no more than that.*[123] (Emphasis in original.)

Such self-awareness will lead to a form of intellectual and political passive resistance, built around the motto of "Do not lie. Do not take part in the lie. Do not support the lie."[124] Arguing that "our country will be purified and transformed without shots and bloodshed," Solzhenitsyn concludes that "this path is also the most moral: we shall be commencing this liberation with *our own souls.*"[125] (Emphasis in original.) Terming his program a "moral revolution," Solzhenitsyn calls upon "my countrymen to engage in purely moral actions, not political ones."[126] "But my programme," he continues, "demands only one thing: the refusal to lie. You must not demonstrate in the streets, you must not take up arms, only don't lie."[127] Solzhenitsyn describes the simplicity and force of this proposal by citing a bus stop encounter evidently narrated to him by one of those present:

A short while ago a group of people were waiting for a bus in Moscow. Suddenly, a slightly tipsy worker said, turning to the others: "And all that Solzhenitsyn tells us is not to applaud." This is precisely it. The very first thing is not to applaud. This in itself will do half the job, because the party bosses will turn dumb once their speeches cease to be supported by applause.[128]

If only "tens or hundreds of thousands, not even millions" were to undertake such passive resistance, Solzhenitsyn feels that "the ruling ideology . . . would collapse, for it would have nothing to stand on."[129]

Initially the province of his "righteous" intelligentsia, this cultural awareness and newfound courage not to lie will gradually spread as others rediscover "'cultural treasures and values' not by erudition, not by scientific accomplishment, *but by our form of spiritual conduct*, laying aside our material well-being and, if the worst comes to the worst, our lives."[130] (Emphasis added.) Solzhenitsyn reminds those who would follow his call to moral revolution that

forming the "backbone of a new people" is not something that can be done as safely and lightheartedly as we are promised [by those dissidents who advocate incremental reforms], at weekends and in our spare time, without giving up our scientific research institutes. No, it will have to be done on weekdays, as part of the mainstream of our life, in its most dangerous sector—and by each one of us in chilling isolation.[131]

These private and chillingly isolated rebirths are likened to a processs of passing society through a "spiritual filter," with each transformation lending added momentum to social and spiritual change and making it just a little easier for those who follow. The rebirth will not be easy, nor will the course necessarily be clear for those who begin the process. "The first tiny minority who set out to force their way through the tight holes of the filter will of their own accord find some new definition of themselves, either while they are still in the filter, or when they have come out the other side and recognized themselves and each other."[132]

It is from among the survivors of this transformation that the new political elite will emerge "to crystallize the people," and it is then from this process of growth and spreading spiritual rebirth that the true Russian people will once again emerge, conscious of their past and of the spiritual and moral values which unite them:

The filter will grow wider and easier for each subsequent particle —and the number of particles passing through it will increase all the time, so that on the far side *these worthy individuals might reconstitute and re-create a worthy people*. . . . So that a society might be reformed whose chief characteristic would be not its level of productivity, nor its degree of prosperity, but *the purity of its social relations.*[133] (Emphasis added.)

THE FUTURE SOCIETY

While many of the elements of social and political change discussed above deal with the nature of the future Russian society that Solzhenitsyn would prefer to see emerge in his homeland, there are other aspects of the interplay of technology and sociopolitical development which cannot be fully portrayed as distinctly social or political events. Such is the case, for example, with his desire to transfer the economic and political center of Russia to the Northeast. While one of the primary motivations is the improvement of the "physical and spiritual health of the people," this relocation of a major portion of the population and the nation's productive capacity is also intended to redefine the fundamental relationship between man and his natural environment on the one hand, and his technological and economic culture on the other. In both spheres, Solzhenitsyn sees this resettlement as the only hope for avoiding eventual decay and self-destruction:

. . . herein lies Russia's hope for winning time and winning salvation: In our Northeastern spaces, which over four centuries our sluggishness has prevented us from multilating by our mistakes, we can build anew; not the senseless, voracious civilization of "progress"—no; we can set up a stable economy without pain or delay and settle people there for the first time according to the needs and principles of that economy. These spaces allow us to hope that we shall not destroy Russia in the general crisis of Western civilization.[134]

Solzhenitsyn is especially concerned with reminding the readers of his *Letter to the Soviet Leaders* of the need for a new environmental and conservationist consciousness. Pointing out that "a dozen worms cannot go on gnawing on the same apple *forever*,"[135] he makes the observation that unrestrained industrial growth and technological modernization have taken place at an exponential rate in the few decades since World War II. Solzhenitsyn accepts without criticism the dire projections of the *Limits to Growth* study and places the blame for the unenviable state of affairs on man's unquestioning acceptance of the notion of material "progress":

When everything is staked on "progress," as it is now, it is *impossible* to find a *joint* optimum solution to all five of the problems referred to above [population, natural resources, agricultural production, industrial growth, and environmental pollution, that is, the Club of Rome's systemic variables]. Unless mankind renounces the notion of economic progress, the biosphere will become unfit for life even *during our lifetime.*[136] (Emphasis in original.)

In the place of the growth-oriented economies of today will arise a zero-growth economy which will serve as the economic and technological manifestations of Solzhenitsyn's basic premise of "self-limitation":

What must be implemented is not a "steadily expanding economy," but a *zero-growth economy*, a stable economy. *Economic growth is not only unnecessary but ruinous*. We must renounce as a matter of urgency, the gigantic scale of modern technology in industry, agriculture and urban development (the cities of today are cancerous tumors). The chief aim of technology will now be to eradicate the lamentable results of previous technologies.[137] (Emphasis in original.)

Going beyond the question of technology itself, Solzhenitsyn also argues that the proper development of the Northeast will reach deeply into the lifestyle and psyche of its inhabitants. One of the principal changes which he recommends is a basic transformation of the nature of urban life:

The urban life which, by now, as much as half our population is doomed to live, is utterly unnatural—and you agree entirely, every one of you [the Soviet leaders, to whom the *Letter* is addressed], for every evening with one accord you all escape from the city to your dachas in the country. And you are all old enough to remember our old towns—towns made for people, horses, dogs—and streetcars too; towns which were humane, friendly, cozy places, where the air was always clean, which were snow-clad in winter and in spring redolent with garden smells. . . . There was a garden to almost every house and hardly a house more than two stories high— the pleasantest height for human habitation. . . . *An economy of nongigantism with small-scale though highly developed technology will not only allow for but necessitate the building of new towns of the old type.* And we can perfectly well set up road barriers at all the entrances and admit horses, and battery-powered electric motors, but not poisonous internal-combustion engines.[138] (Emphasis added.)

Pointing out that a "man's mental and emotional condition is inextricably linked with every aspect of his daily life," Solzhenitsyn argues that the avid pursuit of "progress" and the style of urban life have made man "brutal and cynical." Lamenting the breakdown of the family as a stable social unit, the exploitation of female labor (although he does argue that equal opportunity ought to exist), and the corruption of leisure time by television, cards, and "that same old vodka,"[139] he seems to be calling for a new lifestyle in the "new towns of the old type" that will promote a balance between the spiritual rebirth of his people and their physical well-being, defined in environmental and conservationist terms:

When we set about what, in geographical terms, we shall call the opening up of the Northeast, and, in economic terms, the building of a stable economy . . . *we must also recognize, inherent in all of these aspects, the existence of a moral dimension. The physical and spiritual health of the people must be at the heart of the entire exercise.*[140] (Emphasis added.)

NOTES

1. Alexander I. Solzhenitsyn, *One Day in the Life of Ivan Denisovich* (New York: Fawcett, 1963); *The First Circle* (New York: Harper and Row, 1968); *Gulag Archipelago*, vols. 1–7 (New York: Harper and Row, 1974–78).

2. For the political uses to which the camp literature was put, especially *One Day, see* David Burg and George Feifer, *Solzhenitsyn* (New York: Stein and Day, 1972), pp. 155–80.

3. Alexander I. Solzhenitsyn, *Letter to the Soviet Leaders* (New York:

Harper and Row, 1974); *From Under the Rubble* (Boston: Little, Brown, 1975) (Solzhenitsyn has contributed three essays to this collection: "As Breathing and Consciousness Return," written in 1969 updated in October, 1973, pp. 3–25, "Repentance and Self-Limitation in the Life of Nations," written in November, 1973, pp. 105–43, and "The Smatterers," written in January, 1974, pp. 229–78); *Nobel Lecture* (New York: Farrar, Straus and Giroux, 1972); *Warning to the West* (New York, Farrar, Straus and Giroux, 1976); and *A World Split Apart: Commencement Address Delivered at Harvard University, June 8, 1978* (New York: Harper and Row, 1978).

4. Solzhenitsyn, *Letter*, pp. 11–12.

5. Ibid., pp. 19–20, 23.

6. For discussions of attempts to rationalize and fine tune the economic and administrative machinery of the state, *see* Karl W. Ryavec, *Implementation of Soviet Economic Reforms: Political, Organizational, and Social Processes* (New York: Praeger, 1975); William J. Conyngham, *Industrial Management in the Soviet Union: The Role of the CPSU in Industrial Decision-Making* (Stanford, Calif.: Hoover Institution Press, 1973); and Donald R. Kelley, ed., *Soviet Politics in the Brezhnev Era* (New York: Praeger, 1980).

7. Solzhenitsyn, *Letter*, pp. 22–23.

8. Solzhenitsyn, BBC interview, 1 March 1976, in *Warning to the West*, pp. 114–15.

9. Ibid., p. 106.

10. Ibid., pp. 108–9.

11. Solzhenitsyn, *World Split Apart*, pp. 9–11.

12. Ibid., pp. 33–37.

13. Ibid., pp. 47–49.

14. Ibid.

15. Solzhenitsyn, *Letter*, p. 21.

16. Ibid., pp. 21–22.

17. Solzhenitsyn, "Breathing and Consciouness Return," p. 16.

18. Ibid.

19. Solzhenitsyn, *Gulag Archipelago*, vol. 1, p. 174.

20. Alexander Solzhenitsyn, *Press Conference in Zurich, 16 November 1974* (London, Ontario: Zaria, 1975), pp. 15–16.

21. Alexander I. Solzhenitsyn, "Sakharov and the Criticism of "Letter to the Soviet Leaders,' " in *Kontinent*, eds. Vladimir Maximov et al. (Garden City, N.Y.: Anchor, 1976), p. 18.

22. Solzhenitsyn, *World Split Apart*, p. 33.

23. Ibid., p. 55.

24. Ibid.

25. Solzhenitsyn, *Warning to the West*, p. 41.

26. Alexander I. Solzhenitsyn, "Misconceptions about Russia Are a Threat to America," *Foreign Affairs* 58, no. 4 (Spring 1980), p. 820.

27. Solzhenitsyn, "Breathing and Consciousness Return," p. 12.

28. Solzhenitsyn, *Warning to the West*, pp. 62–64; and "Misconceptions about Russia," p. 816.

29. Solzhenitsyn, "Misconceptions about Russia," p. 820.

30. Ibid.

31. Ibid.

32. Ibid.

33. Solzhenitsyn, *Letter*, p. 7.

34. Ibid., p. 55.

35. Ibid., pp. 27–28.

36. Solzhenitsyn, "Repentance," pp. 140–42.

37. Ibid., pp. 114, 137–38.

38. Solzhenitsyn, *Letter*, pp. 27–28.

39. Ibid., pp. 29–30.

40. Ibid., p. 31.

41. Ibid.

42. Solzhenitsyn, "Repentance," p. 129.

43. Solzhenitsyn, *Letter*, p. 7.

44. Ibid., pp. 30–31.

45. Ibid.; and "Repentance," p. 119.

46. Solzhenitsyn, *Gulag Archipelago*, vols. 5–7, p. 46.

47. Solzhenitsyn, *Gulag Archipelago*, vol. 1, p. 92; vol. 2, pp. 345–46.

48. Solzhenitsyn, "Smatterers," p. 262.

49. Ibid., p. 262.

50. Solzhenitsyn, "Misconceptions about Russia," p. 809.

51. Ibid., p. 811.

52. William Korey, "Sakharov and the Soviet Jewish National Movement," *Midstream* 20, no. 2 (February 1974), pp. 35–46.

53. Solzhenitsyn, "Misconceptions about Russia," p. 816.

54. Solzhenitsyn, "Sakharov and the Criticism," pp. 19–22.

55. Ibid., p. 21.

56. Solzhenitsyn, *Nobel Lecture*, p. 31; and "Repentance," p. 105.

57. Cited in Michael Nicholson, "Solzhenitsyn and *Samizdat*," in *Alexandr Solzhenitsyn: Critical Essays and Documentary Materials*, ed. John B. Dunlop, Richard Haugh, and Alexis Klimoff, 2d ed. (New York: Collier, 1975), p. 63.

58. Solzhenitsyn, *The First Circle*, p. 358.

59. Solzhenitsyn, "Smatterers," p. 245.

60. Ibid., p. 242.

61. Ibid., p. 273.
62. Ibid., p. 234-35.
63. Ibid., p. 268.
64. Alexander Solzhenitsyn, "Matryona's House," in *Stories and Prose Poems* (New York: Bantam, 1971), p. 42.
65. Alexander Solzhenitsyn, *The First Circle*, p. 388.
66. Ibid., p. 389.
67. Solzhenitsyn, "Breathing and Consciousness Return," pp. 19-20.
68. Ibid., p. 5.
69. Solzhenitsyn, "Smatterers," pp. 257-58.
70. Solzhenitsyn, *Nobel Lecture*, pp. 26-27.
71. Quoted by Solzhenitsyn in "Smatterers," pp. 255-57.
72. Ibid.
73. Ibid.
74. Solzhenitsyn, *Warning to the West*, pp. 36-37.
75. Solzhenitsyn, *Letter*, p. 50.
76. Solzhenitsyn, *World Split Apart*, p. 17.
77. Ibid., pp. 17-19.
78. Solzhenitsyn, *Letter*, p. 51.
79. Ibid., pp. 51-52.
80. Solzhenitsyn, "Sakharov and the Criticism," pp. 18-19.
81. Ibid.
82. Solzhenitsyn, "Smatterers," p. 265.
83. Solzhenitsyn, "Breathing and Consciousness Return," p. 17.
84. Solzhenitsyn, *World Split Apart*, pp. 7-9.
85. Solzhenitsyn, "Breathing and Consciousness Return," p. 8.
86. Solzhenitsyn, "Repentance," pp. 135-37.
87. Solzhenitsyn, "Breathing and Consciousness Return," pp. 18-19.
88. Ibid., pp. 22-24.
89. Ibid., pp. 21-22.
90. Ibid.
91. Solzhenitsyn, *Nobel Lecture*, p. 25.
92. Solzhenitsyn, "Breathing and Consciousness Return," p. 18.
93. Ibid., pp. 21-22.
94. Ibid.
95. Solzhenitsyn, *Letter*, p. 51.
96. Solzhenitsyn, "Repentance," p. 136.
97. Ibid., p. 137.
98. Ibid.
99. Solzhenitsyn, *Letter*, p. 52.
100. Ibid.

101. Solzhenitsyn, "Breathing and Consciousness Return," pp. 22–24.
102. Ibid.
103. Ibid., pp. 24–25.
104. Ibid.
105. Solzhenitsyn, *Letter*, p. 53.
106. Solzhenitsyn, "Breathing and Consciousness Return," pp. 24–25.
107. Solzhenitsyn, *Letter*, p. 56.
108. Solzhenitsyn, "Misconceptions about Russia," p. 827.
109. Ibid.
110. Ibid.
111. Ibid.
112. Ibid., p. 828.
113. Ibid., p. 829.
114. Ibid.
115. Solzhenitsyn, *Letter*, p. 56.
116. Ibid., p. 57.
117. Ibid., pp. 54–55.
118. John B. Dunlop, "Solzhenitsyn in Exile," *Survey* 21, no. 3 (Summer 1975), p. 141.
119. Solzhenitsyn, "Repentance," pp. 135–36.
120. Solzhenitsyn, *Nobel Lecture*, p. 22.
121. Solzhenitsyn, *Letter*, pp. 53–54.
122. Solzhenitsyn, "Sakharov and the Criticism," p. 24.
123. Solzhenitsyn, "Breathing and Consciousness Return," p. 25.
124. Solzhenitsyn, "Smatterers," p. 276.
125. Ibid.
126. Solzhenitsyn, *Press Conference in Zurich*, pp. 5–7.
127. Ibid.
128. Ibid.
129. Ibid.
130. Solzhenitsyn, "Smatterers," p. 273.
131. Ibid., p. 272.
132. Ibid., p. 273.
133. Ibid., pp. 273–74.
134. Solzhenitsyn, *Letter*, p. 27.
135. Ibid., p. 21.
136. Ibid., p. 23.
137. Ibid., p. 22.
138. Solzhenitsyn, *Letter*, p. 38.
139. Ibid., pp. 39–41.
140. Ibid., p. 35.

4

Andrei D. Sakharov: An Intellectual Biography

The views of the author were formed in the milieu of the scientific and scientific-technological intelligentsia, which manifests much anxiety over the principles and specific aspects of foreign and domestic policy and over the future of mankind.

Progress, Coexistence, and
Intellectual Freedom

In most ways, the early lives of Andrei D. Sakharov and Alexander I. Solzhenitsyn could not have been more different. While Solzhenitsyn's formal education was ended by the war, Sakharov easily won exemption from military service to continue his studies at Moscow State University. In the immediate postwar years, as Solzhenitsyn was swept into the camps and the ambiguous world of the *sharashka*, Sakharov launched a brilliant career in physics, turning by the end of the decade to secret work on the Soviet hydrogen bomb and deriving both wealth and personal access to the highest elite circles from his contributions to that effort.

Yet, in another sense, the two men were very similar. Each reflected deeply on the significance of his experience, and each ultimately read that experience as mandating a special sense of responsibility and an obligation to speak out on the nature of Soviet society. For Solzhenitsyn, of course, the mission was to speak for the millions who had passed through *Gulag* in silence; his was a message of condemnation and rejection of the fatally flawed system that had produced the "cult of the personality" and a tale that history must not forget. But for Sakharov, the message bore not only a sense of debt for the dangers of nuclear fallout and the hazard of all-out war—although he defends his work on the bomb as necessary—but also a positive vision of a rational and progressive future society consonant with the further peaceful evolution of both socialist and capitalist systems. Just as Solzhenitsyn began his writing career as an emissary of those who had been crushed by the Stalinist system of the past, Sakharov launched his fledgling career as a prophet concerned about the future of mankind in a nuclear world.

Andrei Sakharov is a man uniquely equipped to understand such a nuclear world in all its complexity. Born in Moscow in 1921 into what he has termed "a cultured and close family," Sakharov was the son of a teacher of physics who had authored several well-known texts and popular science works. He completed high school in 1938 and enrolled in Moscow State University, where he was quickly recognized as the most brilliant student of physics in the university's history. When the war began in June, 1941, Sakharov was permitted to continue his studies, a rare exemption from military service which extended even beyond his graduation in the following year. From 1942 to 1945, he worked as an engineer in a war plant, devoting his energies to improving quality control.[1]

After the war, Sakharov returned to his studies. Now working at the Lebedev Institute of Physics under the direction of Igor Tamm, he defended his dissertation in the spring of 1948 and was quickly drawn into a special group that was secretly assigned the task of developing a thermonuclear weapon. "I had no doubts about the vital importance of creating a Soviet superweapon," he recalled in 1973, citing the need for "a balance of power throughout the world" as justification for his actions.[2] He rejects, however, the "father of the hydrogen bomb" appellation which has been used to characterize his efforts and stresses his simultaneous work on the peaceful uses of atomic energy.

Whatever his role, his services were obviously valued by the regime. He was secretly awarded the Stalin Prize and three Orders of Socialist Labor, the highest civilian decoration. He commanded a monthly salary of 2,000 rubles, a sum set specially for him. Moreover, he enjoyed the perquisites of elite status in the Soviet Union that no amount of money can purchase: special housing, a chauffeur-driven automobile, access to restricted resorts and imported consumer goods, and the dubious distinction of having a twenty-four-hour bodyguard. In 1953, at age thirty-two, he was elected a full member of the Soviet Academy of Sciences, the youngest man to be so honored. And throughout those productive years, he was never pressured into joining the party and was specifically exempt from party ideological discipline, a neutrality that is accorded only to truly exceptional and creative individuals.[3]

The "special institutes" within which Sakharov worked from the late 1940s onward left their special mark upon him. While they were filled with the nation's scientific elite, their military mission increasingly made Sakharov ill at ease with the larger implications of his work. Looking backward nearly two decades later, he laments:

Every day I saw the huge material, intellectual, and nervous resources of thousands of people being poured into creating the means of total destruction, a force capable of annihilating all human civilization. I noticed that the control levers were in the hands of people who, although talented in their own way, were cynical. . . . Beginning in the late Fifties, one got an increasingly clearer picture of the collective might of the military-industrial complex and of its vigorous, unprincipled leaders, blind to everything except their "job."[4]

With this growing awareness of the limitations of his political superiors came an increasing sense of personal responsibility for the results of his research. Able to "look upon the whole perverted system as something of an outsider," Sakharov grew even more reflective after the death of Stalin and the Twentieth Party Congress in 1956 when the "cult of the personality" was denounced, and his thoughts turned to "the problems of peace and mankind, and in particular . . . the problems of the thermonuclear war and its aftermath."[5]

The turning point came in 1957. Aware of the growing danger of fallout from nuclear testing and influenced by statements on the matter by prominent scientists and humanitarians such as Linus Pauling and Albert Schweitzer, Sakharov began to feel himself "responsible for the problem of radioactive contamination from nuclear explosions."[6] Taking advantage of his unique position in the Soviet hierarchy, he became a crusader for a cessation of further testing and a proponent of a test-ban treaty with the Americans. The task was not easy; he was countered at virtually every turn both by the cynical lack of concern on the part of political authorities at the highest level and by the real, if flawed, view that nuclear fallout was a price that had to be paid for the development of the Soviet weapons program. Sakharov wrote numerous memoranda on the topic that circulated within the very limited confines of the nuclear establishment and spoke of his concern at conferences of fellow scientists. In 1958, he convinced I. V. Kurchatov, the director of the nuclear weapons program, that a scheduled series of tests was unnecessary, but Kurchatov's personal intercession with Khrushchev to cancel the tests fell on deaf ears, and they were conducted.[7]

Sakharov's opposition to testing continued, and in 1961, at an informal meeting between Khrushchev and top nuclear scientists, he carried his case directly to the First Secretary. When the scientists were instructed to prepare for a new round of tests designed principally to impress the West with Soviet strength, Sakharov quickly penned a note to Khrushchev expressing his opposition. "To resume tests after a three-year moratorium," he wrote, "would undermine the talks on banning tests and on disarmament, and would lead to a new round in the armaments race. . . ."[8] He passed the note up the table to Khrushchev, who put it in his pocket without reading it. In an off-the-cuff speech later that same evening, the First Secretary responded frankly to the implications of Sakharov's challenge, arguing that Soviet policy toward the United States must be conducted from a "position of strength" and that the "tricky business" of making foreign policy ought to be left to the politicians.[9]

Sakharov continued his opposition the following year in response to a decision by the Ministry of Medium Machine Building—
the transparent "official" designation of the Soviet nuclear weapons
program—to authorize a routine test that he regarded as technically
unnecessary. His attempts to influence his superiors to cancel the
test were drawn out over several tension-filled weeks. On the eve
of the test, Sakharov called the top official of the nuclear weapons
program and threatened to resign, only to receive a clear message
that his talents were now regarded as dispensable. He then put
through a hurried call to Khrushchev, who was in Ashkhabad,
and urged him to intervene. Pretending ignorance, the First Secretary promised to look into the matter and get back in touch with
Sakharov. When the return call came the following day, it was
from a Khrushchev aide, and informed Sakharov that the test
schedule had been advanced; in fact, the test had occurred shortly
before the return call.[10]

Sakharov was crushed both by his failure to prevent the test
and by the obvious deception by the authorities. Having already
concluded that such tests were "criminal," he took the next step in
his growing disaffection with the regime. "I had an awful sense of
powerlessness. I could not stop something that I knew was wrong
and unnecessary. After that, I felt myself another man. I broke
with my surroundings. It was a basic break. After that, I understood that there was no point in arguing."[11]

While he still opposed further tests, Sakharov altered his tactics
immediately following this abortive attempt in 1962 to convince
Khrushchev to cancel an unnecessary explosion. On a visit to the
minister in charge of the nuclear program to discuss the long-
standing stalemate in Soviet-American test-ban talks caused by
the inability of either side to detect underground tests, he pointed
out that a previous American fallback proposal offered in 1959 had
attempted to sidestep the issue by suggesting a ban on such tests
in the atmosphere, in space, and in any of the world's oceans,
environments in which monitoring was no problem. When a year
later such a pact was formally concluded following these general
outlines, Sakharov permitted himself to conclude that "it was
possible that my initiative was of help in this historic act."[12]

While the questions of arms policy and fallout had been the catalysts of Sakharov's new political awareness, his attention quickly spread to other issues. As he told Hedrick Smith in 1973, "the atomic question was always half science, half politics. The atomic issue was a natural path into political issues. What matters is that I left conformism. It is not important on what question. After that first break, everything later was natural."[13]

Two other issues outside of the purview of nuclear weapons policy also animated Sakharov in this period. One was the educational reform of 1958, which initially envisioned the addition of polytechnical work-study programs in the last years of a student's secondary education, and a period of direct service in industry before entry into advanced education. Noting the course of his own career (obviously without going into the substantive details), Sakharov publicly opposed such practical distractions for the most gifted students in the natural sciences, arguing that the most productive years occur in the early twenties. His argument seemingly carried some weight—although he was not alone in making the point—and the subsequent reforms handed down late in the year provided for special schools for students gifted in the sciences and for their direct entry into higher educational institutions.[14]

Even more politically significant was Sakharov's entry into the continuing dispute about the dubious impact of Trofim Lysenko on Soviet genetics. By all accounts, Lysenko was a palpable charlatan, who had sold Stalin a flawed theory of genetics that provided the theoretical groundwork for the rapid malleability of all biological forms and who had, more ominously, drawn upon Stalin's endorsement to purge his opponents from scientific and academic circles. Even though Lysenkoism had fallen upon hard times immediately after the *Vozhd*'s death, it enjoyed a brief respite under Khrushchev, whose propensity to seek rapid solutions to intractable problems in agriculture fell into line with Lysenko's assumption that rapid genetic changes were possible. Twice Sakharov struck against the bogus theory, once directly against an abortive attempt to resurrect Lysenko's most questionable theories in the early 1960s, and once against the nomination of Nikolai Nuzhdin, a close Lysenko associate, for full membership in the Academy of Sciences. In the latter case, he was joined by many other noted scientists who were resentful of Lysenko's pseudopolitical role, and the nomination was rejected. Carrying his opposition a step further, he then spoke out against the conferring of academic rank on the party's agricultural spokesman, S. P. Trapeznikov; the move angered Khrushchev, who apparently ordered the KGB "to teach Sakharov a lesson" shortly before his fall in October, 1964. Khrushchev's removal from office in October, 1964, cut short such reprisals, and Trapeznikov subsequently rose to the position of the party's overseer of scientific research.[15]

Such opposition was not without penalty, however. For the first time, Sakharov was publicly attacked by the president of the Academy of Agricultural Sciences, and he suffered a notable decline in terms of his status within the privileged community of leading scientists. His security clearance was reduced by several grades, and, as a consequence, he began to write about the more global questions of quark phenomena and the expanding universe. Perhaps even more significantly, by the mid 1960s he had relocated to Moscow, leaving the closed nuclear community of Turkmenia far behind, and had begun to exchange ideas with other scientists and potential dissidents, including the newly famous author, Alexander Solzhenitsyn. As he later put it, these years had "great psychological significance" and "expanded the circle of persons with whom I associated."[16] No less importantly, these years carried him into the mainstream of the emerging *samizdat* network, which brought both new friends and new ideas.

Two influential new friends were the Medvedev brothers, Zhores and Roy. The former's essay on the rise and fall of Lysenkoism was the first *samizdat* item that Sakharov read, and the latter's clandestine history of the Stalin years had a deep effect on him. Whatever their subsequent differences, Sakharov still maintains that he "cannot minimize their role in my own development."[17]

The mid 1960s also witnessed an escalation in Sakharov's willingness to confront the regime directly over purely political issues not associated with nuclear policy. In 1966, he was one of the more prominent signers of a letter to the Twenty-Third Party Congress warning against any rehabilitation of Stalin. In the same year, he also wrote to the Supreme Soviet to oppose legislation that would strengthen the hand of the regime against dissidents, and directly to Brezhnev to protest the arrest of four leading critics.[18]

The next several years saw the birth of a new strain in Sakharov's writings—what he has termed his "futurological" works dealing both with the problems that retard the forces of "progress" and with the nature of a future, more perfect world. In 1967, he penned a brief piece about the role of science in society which circulated in limited edition within the scientific community. He also co-authored an article on the nature of the intelligentsia and the threat of thermonuclear war for *Literaturnaya Gazeta*, and although censors blocked publication, it circulated in the growing *samizdat* network. Both of these works figured importantly in the development in the following year of Sakharov's first major volume, *Progress, Coexistence, and Intellectual Freedom*, which brought him to the respectful attention of Western audiences and focused the less than respectful light of KGB attention on his activities.[19]

Sakharov readily admits that the "general tenor of the work was affected by the time of its writing—the height of the 'Prague Spring,'" a period of hope and optimism for many within the dissident community. In this volume, he offered "a compilation of liberal, humanistic, and 'scientocratic' ideas based on information available to me and on personal experience." While he today regards this work as "eclectic, pretentious in places, and imperfect ('raw') in terms of form," he nonetheless confesses that "its basic ideas are dear to me."[20]

His thoughts were clearly not so dear to Soviet officials, who removed Sakharov from all secret projects in August, 1968, and permitted him to sink to the post of a researcher at the Physics Institute of the Soviet Academy of Sciences, the place where he had studied with Igor Tamm years before, and the lowest ranking post that an Academy member could hold. These changes "resulted in the restructuring of my entire way of life," Sakharov has reported, and while free to conduct nonclassified research at the institute, he rapidly found himself now incapable of truly significant and creative endeavors, in part because he had already passed his prime in the youth-dominated field of theoretical physics and in part because of the increasing stresses placed on his life by his activities as a dissident and the death of his first wife in 1969.[21]

In the early 1970s, Sakharov openly crossed over the line that separates in-house critics and pamphleteers from open and militant dissidents. The events that occasioned the shift had less to do with his own fate than with the increasingly strident repression of his new allies within the dissident movement. Beginning in 1970, the regime struck hard against its critics, bringing some before staged trials and committing others to mental institutions. With each arrest or incarceration came a new series of protests or public vigils, and Sakharov joined in signing the petitions or in standing the vigils during trials. In October, 1970, he was given passes to attend the political trial of a relatively minor dissident figure—in such trials, the "open" courtroom would either be packed in advance with a hostile audience or such passes would be required—although it is not clear whether such clearance was a reward for past contributions or an invitation to view into his own possible future. In either case, by the autumn of the following year, he was now systematically excluded from such trials and always found himself on the wrong side of a line of "volunteer" guards who were assigned to control access to the court. The once insider, the man who could pass Khrushchev a note or use a special phone to call him anywhere in the nation, was now the outsider looking in.[22]

Like Solzhenitsyn, Sakharov also came at this point in his life to perceive a "debt too great to be repaid to the brave and good people who are incarcerated in prisons, camps, and psychiatric hospitals."[23] As his contacts within the dissident community multiplied in the early 1970s, and especially as he increasingly came into contact with rank and file dissidents who lacked prominence and international reputations to protect them from outright arrest or "administrative measures," he came to appreciate both the sheer courage that it took for an ordinary citizen to stand up before the regime, and the overriding importance of the issue of human rights as the central, unifying theme for the movement. In Sakharov's view, morality and law were to form a common ethical standard which provided the philosophical basis for "the systematic defense of human rights and ideals and not a political struggle, which would inevitably incite people to violence, sectarianism, and frenzy."[24] He sees the apolitical role of Amnesty International as the model for such action within the Soviet Union, and he collaborated with other leading dissidents in the creation of the Initiative Group for the Defense of Human Rights and the somewhat later and more aggressive Human Rights Committee.[25]

Throughout the remainder of the decade, Sakharov increasingly became the most visible lightning rod of the dissident movement. As repression tightened, his own views grew increasingly more strident in opposition to the regime and less optimistic about hopes for the sort of peaceful reforms envisioned in his 1968 memorandum. With each important new work, the tone hardened perceptibly, and Sakharov became ever more concerned with the defense of individual dissidents and whole peoples who had been the victims of repression. He continued to write directly to top Soviet leaders to condemn repressive measures or to argue for progressive reforms, but even by the middle of the decade, he had already begun to refer to much of earlier programmatic statements as wistful "optimistic futurology."[26]

Sakharov's own personal life also bore the marks of his dissident status. On the one hand, his forthrightness and sheer courage to stand up against the regime had brought a host of new friends and supporters within the dissident community itself, and it is evident from his writings about those figures such as the Medvedev brothers, Pyotr Grigorenko, and a long list of others that this diverse assortment had a profound effect upon the previously cloistered physicist. His activities as a dissident also brought him a new wife—Yelena Bonner, a long-time dissident in her own right, whom he met in 1970 while standing vigil outside a courtroom where a dissident was on trial.[27]

But, on the other hand, his status as one of the most open and combative of the dissidents—it must be remembered that perhaps an even more prominent figure, Solzhenitsyn, carefully harbored his time and energies, letting Sakharov and others carry the battle to the enemy and bear the brunt of the predictable retaliation—cost him an exacting price. Not the least of his worries was the increasing pressure from the regime itself, which in 1972–73 began a headlong attack on the dissident community. Even his continued professional role as a researcher at the Lebedev Institute was reduced to a mockery (although some Soviet physicists and a growing number of foreign scientists attempted to sustain a sort of floating seminar in which dissident scientists could maintain contact with the latest developments in their fields), and direct public attacks against him were launched as early as 1973. Even more insidiously, both his own growing frustration and the quiet but ever-present harassment of the regime took a costlier toll. While his new marriage united two souls in common cause, it also brought its own special pain; Sakharov has become estranged from the three children of his first marriage, and Yelena Bonner's children have suffered predictable penalties such as expulsion from university or other such "administrative" sanctions. More ominously, the regime has struck directly at Bonner herself, both interrogating her at great length as a way of putting pressure on Sakharov and then denying her the opportunity to receive treatment abroad for an eye ailment, although it eventually relented on the latter measure, probably as a result of the outcry in the West.[28]

In August, 1973, Sakharov received the first of a series of formal warnings that a continuation of his dissident activities could bring prosecution under Soviet law. He was summoned to a meeting with Mikhail P. Malyarov, the Procuracy's first deputy prosecutor, and reminded that years before as a nuclear physicist working on top-secret projects, he had signed a pledge not to reveal state secrets or to meet with foreigners. Arguing that the pledge was still in force even though Sakharov no longer labored on defense projects and that his meetings with foreigners were used to pass slanderous materials to the West for publication—an act itself punishable under Articles 190–91 of the criminal code—Malyarov invited the physicist "to consider this a serious warning and to draw your conclusions."[29]

In 1975, Sakharov's second comprehensive essay, *My Country and the World*, circulated in *samizdat* form within the Soviet Union and was published in the West. While it retained much of the internationalist and cosmopolitan flavor of his earlier works, especially concerning the need for worldwide and progressive reforms, it nonetheless clearly reflected his new pessimism. Soviet society was portrayed as less malleable and capable of internal reform than in the 1968 memorandum, and, perhaps more importantly, Sakharov's view of the West had changed perceptibly. Although he still held out hope that the positive features of Western society—its openness, pluralism, and willingness to permit scientific progress—will remain, he questioned whether it will have the power to meet the growing Soviet challenge, both in terms of guaranteeing its supremacy in a competitive world and its willingness to place pressure on totalitarian systems to grant even the most basic human rights to their citizens.[30]

In October, 1975, Sakharov's spirits were raised by his designation as the recipient of the Nobel Peace Prize, making him the second major dissident figure to be honored by the Nobel Committee within five years. For their part, Norwegian officials attempted to mollify Soviet officials and raised no outcry when Sakharov was denied a visa to attend the awards ceremony. Yelena Bonner, who was in Italy for medical treatment, instead journeyed to Oslo to accept the prize and read the Nobel lecture in her husband's absence. Characteristically, Sakharov himself attended a political trial in Lithuania at the time of the ceremony, although he and other dissidents were barred from the courtroom.[31]

The following year was marked by vigorous attempts by Sakharov and other dissidents to mobilize international public opinion against Soviet repression of dissidents. Now more confident of his standing in the eyes of a world audience, Sakharov lent his name to numerous appeals to organizations such as Amnesty International, the International League of Human Rights, and even the European Conference of Communist Parties, held in East Berlin in June, 1976, during the brief ascendancy of Eurocommunism as a viable and largely anti-Soviet movement, at least on the human rights issue. These measures had little impact on the fate of dissidents, although they were important in focusing increasing foreign attention on Soviet repression.[32]

Although disappointed with the results of his appeals to international bodies and foreign leaders since his Nobel award, Sakharov turned with great hope to the American presidential election, addressing an appeal for support to both Ford and Carter in October, 1976. The day after Carter won the election, Sakharov cabled his congratulations and gratitude for Carter's "unambiguous statements in defense of human rights throughout the world."[33] The first concrete appeal for support came on January 3, 1977, even before the new administration had assumed office, as a re-. sult of the conviction of Pyotr Rubin, a minor dissident figure who had received eight years in the camps for advocating Ukrainian secession.[34]

Sakharov's appeals to the Carter administration took a more serious turn nearly three weeks later when circumstances permitted him to compose what he had thought would be a private letter to the new president. For Sakharov, the offer of Martin Garbus, an American lawyer in Moscow seeking to discuss the fate of certain Jewish dissidents with Soviet authorities, to carry a letter to Carter presented him with an opportunity both to establish direct contact with the new president and to deny rumors circulating in the West that frustrated elements of the dissident community had turned to violence, including a recent subway bombing in Moscow. Hastily written and poorly translated, the letter merely reiterated Sakharov's hope that the president would speak out in defense of dissidents not only in the USSR but also in the repressive nations of Eastern Europe and provided a list of those individuals then most in peril. On his return to the United States, Garbus simultaneously conveyed the letter to State Department officials and released it to the *New York Times* and the *Los Angeles Times*.[35] On February 2, Sakharov told a *Newsweek* interviewer in Moscow that he had intended the letter to be a private communication, although he added that both publicity and pressure from abroad were necessary parts of the dissidents' strategy, themes which he again stressed in a CBS interview on February 10.[36] Exactly a week later, Sakharov was summoned to the American embassy to receive a direct reply from Carter, who expressed his continued willingness "to use our good offices to seek the release of prisoners of conscience," although no mention was made of the fate of the specific dissidents cited in Sakharov's earlier communication. Sakharov immediately released the Carter letter to the press and the same day penned a response thanking the president for his support and adding to the previous list of endangered dissidents the names of Alexander Ginzberg, Mykola Rudenko, Oleksei

Tykhy, and Yuri Orlov, who had been arrested in February in a crackdown on the various Helsinki Watch Groups.[37]

The timing of Carter's support could not have been more propitious. Since mid January, dissidents had lived with the growing fear that the subway bombing incident would become the *cause célèbre*—"the Reichstag fire," as one of them put it—to justify even more strident repression. Rumors spread among the dissidents that the arrests of the Helsinki Watch Group members and other critics were the first wave of a new campaign to suppress the movement. Official attention first centered on Vladimir Rubtsov, an electrician by profession and a minor figure within the dissident community, who was interrogated concerning his activities on the day of the blast. But his ties to other, more significant critics were ominously clear: Rubtsov was a close friend of Efrem Yankelevich, Sakharov's son-in-law through his marriage to Bonner. On January 18, Sakharov called Western correspondents to his apartment to receive a statement concerning Rubtsov's interrogation and its larger implications. Exactly a week later, on January 25, Sakharov was himself summoned to the Procuracy in Moscow to hear a warning against any further slander of "the organs of state security," which he suggested had acted as an *agent provocateur* in staging the blast. Sakharov refused to countersign the document to indicate that he acknowledged the warning and instead quickly called a press conference to denounce this latest action.[38] The matter was far from ended, however. A press campaign against the "slanderer" Sakharov was quickly launched, including a piece accepted for publication on the "Op Ed" page of the *New York Times*.[39] In mid February, additional pressure was applied through the interrogation of Efrem Yankelevich concerning the bombing, although no formal indictment was filed. By the early summer of 1977, the furor had died down, and it was not until June of the following year that Soviet officials announced that they had arrested several individuals in connection with the explosion, with no indication that the act had been linked to dissidents.[40]

Over the next two years, the authorities continued their harassment of Sakharov and his family. Until their emigration to the United States late in 1977, the Yankelevich family took the most serious blows, which ranged from petty harassment and periodic interrogation to direct threats of criminal prosecution for their dissident activities; one abortive attempt was even made to link Efrem with an auto accident, an offense which usually brings severe criminal sanctions from Soviet courts. With their departure, attention fell on Alexsei Semyonov, Bonner's son by a previous marriage whom Sakharov now treated as his own offspring. In November, 1977, he was expelled from a Moscow pedagogical school on trumped-up charges that he had "violated military discipline" in a required military preparedness course.[41]

Both the direct attacks on Sakharov, which continued after the subway bombing incident, and the continuing harassment of his family exacted an increasing price in terms of his personal life and composure. Bonner herself remained a target of officially inspired attacks, which accused her of intensifying her own activities as repayment for the "thirty pieces of silver" that she allegedly received from unnamed sources in the West during her medical treatment in Italy and portrayed her as the "evil genius" behind her husband's acts.[42] Sakharov himself lost his usual composure in April, 1976, while attempting to attend the trial of a spokesman of the Crimean Tatars in Omsk. Involved in an increasingly violent shoving incident between would-be spectators and the local police outside the courtroom and sensing himself and his wife to be special targets of the attack, he struck a KGB agent and a local policeman. The pair was briefly detained at the local police station, but no formal charges were ever brought against them, although the fear of prosecution hung over their heads for a number of months.[43]

By the end of 1976, Sakharov began to speak openly to Western correspondents about the impact of his activities on his personal life. "I am beginning to feel the strain after so many years of public activity for which I was psychologically ill prepared," he told an Associated Press correspondent in December, continuing that "it was psychologically very difficult for me to bear the burden of world fame."[44] Confessing that his personal situation and that of his family "is getting worse year after year and could worsen even further," he described a lifestyle marked by growing frustration and isolation. "I live day by day, doing what life requires of me. How long that can continue depends on many factors, both personal and public. It depends in part upon the help that I receive—on how younger men take on themselves the responsibilities I carry, and in part upon the support I get from world public opinion."[45]

Despite his growing pessimism, he took great interest in the approaching conference of the thirty-five nations that had signed the Helsinki accords, which was to meet in Belgrade in October, 1977. Soviet compliance with the provisions of the so-called basket three human rights agreements had been virtually nonexistent; the Helsinki Watch Groups had been effectively crushed and their leaders sent to the camps, confined to psychiatric care, or driven abroad. In such a setting, the only feasible strategy was to turn to the West for support. In the months before the meeting, Sakharov addressed numerous appeals to Western and communist leaders alike to condemn Soviet actions, especially the severe criminal sanctions that were threatened against Helsinki Watch Group leaders and the increasing level of violence being applied to silence less prominent figures. Whether as a result of these appeals or simply out of cosmetic motivations of their own, Soviet leaders did briefly suspend the trials of the Watch Group members shortly before the conference. The respite was brief, however; the conference itself failed to produce a ringing denunciation of repression—even the American delegation now reflected a more "balanced" position, signaling a shift in the administration's position—and the trials quickly resumed after the adjournment.[46]

Sakharov's appeals to the West quickly brought another round of denunciations in the Soviet press. Ominously the officially inspired condemnations warned of possible criminal sanctions for "antipatriotic and antisocial activities which frequently contradict Soviet law."[47] From the West, however, came new signs of support. In November, 1977, Sakharov and Anatoly Shcharansky were named as corecipients of the Joseph Prize for Human Rights awarded by the Anti-Defamation League of the B'nai B'rith, and later that same month, Sakharov was invited to speak before the annual meeting of the strongly anticommunist AFL-CIO, which had previously honored Solzhenitsyn in a similar manner. Unable to attend, he sent a speech that openly suggested that the huge union apply pressure to the now-wavering Carter administration to reaffirm its commitment to human rights.[48]

The next two years brought more of the same. As the regime struck more intensely against lesser dissident figures and ignored Western appeals for the release or negotiated expatriation of already imprisoned figures such as Orlov and Shcharansky, Sakharov increasingly emerged as the remaining dominent figure still active within the movement. Although he denied that he had become "a general without an army," his isolation within his homeland visibly increased in 1978 and 1979. Perhaps even more frightening was the seeming reduction of visible support from the West. While the Carter administration continued to express its *pro forma* support of prisoners of conscience wherever they might be, in practical terms it had shifted emphasis to more conventional diplomatic dealings with the Soviet Union and had begun to prepare itself for a protracted internal debate over the ratification of the SALT II accords. The major European powers, which had only grudgingly supported the human rights aspects of the Helsinki agreements, anxiously focused their attention on the economic benefits of détente rather than on the potentially disruptive question of the treatment of dissidents. The much-touted Eurocommunist movement, to which dissidents in the Soviet Union and Eastern Europe alike had looked with great hope for the emergence of a tolerant and "human" socialism, also came upon hard times at the close of the decade, falling victim either to electoral reversals or to long-standing feuds within the respective national parties or with coalition allies.[49]

The summer and autumn of 1979 witnessed even more strident attacks on dissidents, in part in an attempt to sweep them from the scene before the summer Olympics the following year, and in part as a consequence of the rapid deterioration of Soviet-American relations. While the central issue of the latter was the Kremlin's perception that the Carter administration did not have the political skill—or more ominously, simply did not intend—to secure Senate ratification of SALT II, the distrust and mutual recriminations spilled over to poison other policy issues. Perceiving that little was still to be gained by staying their hand against dissidents as a tacit quid pro quo of the now-doubtful ratification of the agreement, Soviet leaders simply wrote off the prospects for a successful conclusion of the pact in the near future and moved instead to crack down on their own internal critics, undoubtedly reasoning that such actions would do little to worsen an already fractured relationship.

Throughout the intensification of repressive measures from the summer onward, Sakharov continued to speak out in defense of fellow dissidents and to report the over forty arrests and trials to Western audiences. Initially the authorities seemed unsure of how to deal with this new spate of activities. On the one hand, they went to considerable measures to prevent him from attending an otherwise tame panel on human rights at the International Political Science Association meeting in Moscow in August. But on the other hand, they did little to prevent Western and third-world scholars attending the meeting from journeying to his apartment, where he conducted what amounted to a running seminar for several days.[50]

After the Soviet invasion of Afghanistan in December, attitudes and postures stiffened on both sides on the confrontation. For his part, Sakharov condemned the Soviet action as blatant agression and supported the Carter administration's call for direct sanctions against the USSR and a boycott of the summer Olympics. Now virtually the only internationally known dissident figure still at liberty within the Soviet Union, he took the lead within the small dissident community in criticizing the invasion and in warning the West about the further dangers of one-sided détente.[51]

For nearly a month after the December invasion, the regime maintained its silence; routine harassment continued, but there were no special new measures or blatant threats of official retaliation. Then on January 22, 1980, it struck with swift effectiveness. Intercepted on his way to a weekly meeting at the Academy of Sciences, Sakharov was taken before Deputy Prosecutor General Alexander Rekunkov, who informed him of a special decree stripping him of awards and decorations and exiling him to Gorky, an industrial city some 250 miles from Moscow and off limits to foreigners. He was permitted to call his wife, who was to share internal exile with him, although no charges had been brought against her. Less than four hours after he had left his Moscow apartment, Sakharov and Bonner were placed aboard a special plane and transported to obviously carefully prepared quarters in the closed provincial city. They carried with them only a few belongings that Bonner, notified by telephone in mid afternoon of their fate, had been able to pack in two suitcases. Ruf Bonner, Yelena's mother, who had been at the couple's apartment when the call came, expressed the stunned reaction of all who heard the news: "We did not have time for goodbyes. . . . Suddenly they were gone."[52]

Sakharov's life in Gorky has been one of quiet frustration and nearly total isolation. The couple resides in a small apartment under the constant surveillance of the KGB. The entrance is guarded day and night by a uniformed police officer, the phones are tapped, and special short-wave jamming facilities to prevent radio reception have been set up nearby. The few friends or colleagues who occasionally visit are interrogated upon their departure, and Sakharov himself must periodically report to the authorities. Although he attempts to occupy his time with scientific endeavors, he suffers from a deep sense of professional isolation; only on one occasion have his colleagues from the Institute of Physics been permitted to visit him, and contact with others outside the Soviet Union has been cut off. His only remaining channel of communication with the West is through Bonner's periodic trips to Moscow to meet with foreign correspondents. Since technically she has not been confined to the Gorky area, she is free to travel as frequently as she pleases, although she too is always under the watchful eye of the KGB on such occasions, and the authorities have informed her mother that they may "take certain measures" if such trips are used to thwart her husband's isolation. Since he regards his internal exile as illegal, Sakharov has challenged the authorities to bring him to trial on formal charges or to permit him to emigrate, an option that he once opposed but now hints he would accept.[53]

In exile, Sakharov has grown even more pessimistic about the prospects for his homeland and the fate of the dissident movement, at least for the next decade. While he maintains hope that eventually "the more responsible, non-dogmatic members of the Soviet leadership" will step forward with meaningful reforms,[54] and that active dissent "will continue in one form or another, whatever the size of the movement," he sees the immediate future a period of "ever greater repression."[55] "Everything is," he concludes, "as it was under . . . Stalin," except that now, despite the pressures and the risks, the Sakharovs are heard.[56]

NOTES

1. Andrei D. Sakharov, "How I Came to Dissent," *New York Review of Books,* 21 March 1974, pp. 11-17; Hedrick Smith, "The Intolerable Andrei Sakharov," *New York Times Magazine,* 4 November 1973, pp. 42-64; and Sakharov's own biographical statement in *Sakahrov Speaks,* ed. Harrison E. Salisbury (New York: Vintage, 1974), pp. 29-54.

2. Sakharov, "How I Came to Dissent," p. 11.

3. Harrison E. Salisbury, "Foreword," in Salisbury, *Sakharov Speaks,* p. 5.

4. Sakharov, "How I Came to Dissent," p. 11.

5. Ibid.

6. Ibid.

7. Ibid.

8. Ibid.

9. Ibid.

10. Ibid.

11. Ibid.

12. Smith, "Intolerable Andrei Sakharov," p. 56.

13. Sakharov, "How I Came to Dissent," p. 11.

14. Smith, "Intolerable Andrei Sakharov," p. 56.

15. Salisbury, *Sakharov Speaks,* pp. 10-11.

16. Ibid., pp. 13-14.

17. Sakharov, "How I Came to Dissent," p. 12.

18. Ibid.

19. Ibid.

20. Andrei D. Sakharov, *Progress, Coexistence, and Intellectual Freedom* (New York: Norton, 1968).

21. Ibid.

22. Ibid.

23. Ibid., p. 14.

24. Ibid.

25. Ibid., pp. 14-15.

26. Andrei D. Sakharov, *My Country and the World* (New York: Vintage, 1975), p. 5.

27. Smith, "Intolerable Andrei Sakharov," p. 61.

28. Andrei D. Sakharov, *Alarm and Hope* (New York: Vintage, 1978), p. 18.

29. Andrei D. Sakharov, "Interview with Mikhail P. Malyarov, First Deputy Soviet Prosecutor, August 16, 1973," cited in Salisbury, *Sakharov Speaks*, p. 184.

30. Sakharov, *My Country*, especially pp. 99–109.

31. Sakharov, *Alarm and Hope*, p. 18.

32. Ibid., pp. 28–36.

33. Ibid., p. 44.

34. Ibid., p. 42.

35. Ibid., p. 46.

36. Ibid., pp. 48–49.

37. Ibid., p. 50–52.

38. Ibid., p. 68–72.

39. *New York Times*, February 23, 1978, p. 27.

40. Sakharov, *Alarm and Hope*, p. 80.

41. Ibid., p. 97.

42. Ibid., p. 89–90.

43. Ibid., pp. 87–88.

44. Ibid., p. 84.

45. Ibid., p. 92.

46. Ibid., p. 150–54.

47. Ibid., p. 159.

48. Ibid., pp. 162–67.

49. *New York Times*, 16 January 1978, p. 2, and 31 March 1978, p. 8.

50. *New York Times*, 27 January 1979, IV p. 2.

51. Andrei D. Sakharov, "A Letter from Exile," *New York Times Magazine*, 8 June 1980, p. 33.

52. *New York Times*, 23 January 1980, p. 10.

53. Sakharov, "A Letter from Exile," p. 111.

54. Ibid., p. 33.

55. Ibid., p. 106.

56. Ibid., p. 80.

5

Andrei D. Sakharov and the Rational Social Order

Given his training and his previous career experience as well as his initial concern with the global consequences of nuclear testing, it is hardly surprising that Andrei D. Sakharov's increasingly critical attitude toward the repressive policies of the Soviet regime would stress the dual—and in his mind, inseparable—themes of a rationally governed society and an international approach to solving both domestic and world problems. Underpinning both strains of thought is a commitment to a vaguely defined sense of "progress," conceived of both as an inevitable and salutary growth and further modernization of science and technology *writ large*, and as a concomitant rationalization and democratization of the social order. Yet weighing against these trends are the foreboding threat of nuclear war, which Sakharov views as a distinct possibility, and the division of the world into competing blocs. Writing in 1977, he noted that of all the problems of the modern world, "foremost among them [is] the threat of universal destruction in a major nuclear war," a situation "created and aggravated by the division of humanity into opposing capitalist and socialist systems and into the Third World of developing countries."[1] Yet for Sakharov, "peace, progress, and human rights . . . are indissolubly linked: it is impossible to achieve one of them if the others are ignored."[2]

POLITICAL AND SOCIAL LEGITIMACY

In contrast to Solzhenitsyn's view of an organic social order rooted in tradition, Sakharov sees Soviet society as merely a retarded example of the "progressive" worldwide process of industrialization and social differentiation. Industrial development and technological modernization are viewed as positive features of any modern society, and Sakharov is optimistic about the future of his homeland *if* these forces are permitted to develop rationally. In such a setting, the keys to social and political legitimacy lie in the functional and "progressive" roles performed by various social elements. To Sakharov, the glue that binds society together is the common acceptance of the rational integration of its many functionally specialized parts and the acknowledgment of the positive value of a loosely defined sense of "progress." While he acknowledges that his ideas were formed "in the milieu of the scientific and scientific-technological intelligentsia," he maintains that they have strong humanistic overtones since his concept of progress includes not only technological and economic advances, but also the creation of a social order devoted to the protection of individual freedom and the general public welfare.[3]

Sakharov defines his notions of social and political legitimacy in terms of specific attitudes toward progress and the presence of talents and skills presumably needed by that future society, rather than in terms of institutional structures and mechanisms of public choice by which social and political leadership will emerge. In his mind, legitimacy emerges as a consequence of accepting four interwoven themes of development and social transformation: (1) the desirability of scientific and technological progress as the driving forces of social and political evolution, (2) the acceptance of a rationally planned social and economic order, (3) the democratization of the political system, with special emphasis on the involvement of groups that possess special skills needed by advanced, technologically sophisticated industrial societies, and (4) the convergence (as he puts it, the "socialist" convergence) of all mature industrial systems.

The sense of social purpose and national identity which Solzhenitsyn found in Russia's historical past is for Sakharov derived from the notion of continuing technological and social progress toward a completely rationalized society. Thus, particular events or social forces are evaluated in terms of their ability to contribute to or to retard the emergence of this future idealized state, and political and social legitimacy rest ultimately in the hands of those elements of the scientific and technical elite that function as the "carriers" of this sense of modernity. It is in this vein that Sakharov bitterly criticizes both Solzhenitsyn's desire for a traditional moral order and an organic society (that is, regressive steps) and contemporary restrictions on political life and intellectual freedom (that is, limitations on the further development of scientific inquiry), for each in its own way slows the further rationalization of society.

Focusing his attention on the present Soviet leadership, Sakharov argues that they have lacked the foresight and the courage to develop a mature and technologically sophisticated society. His most sweeping criticism is that they have failed to enter into the "second industrial revolution" now current in the West. Because of restrictions on the free exchange of information and other "antidemocratic traditions," the Soviet Union has not yet begun to build what Western analysts have termed a "post-industrial" society, that is, a technologically sophisticated social order dependent on knowledge-intensive industries, computerization, advanced technology, and in which social and political power allegedly shift from the hands of former political elites to those of the new manager-technocrats. While Solzhenitsyn has interpreted this tendency to lag behind the West in technological matters as a positive and hopeful phenomenon, Sakharov views it as merely another indication that Soviet leaders have failed in their efforts to build a modern society.[4]

Sakharov is no less critical of Solzhenitsyn's "tragic" view of technology. While he acknowledges the warnings of Norbert Weiner and others concerning the antihumanist possibilities inherent in technological advances, he maintains that further progress is both inevitable and desirable:

Population growth and the depletion of natural resources make *it absolutely impossible for mankind to return to the so-called healthy life of that past (which was, in reality, very difficult and often cruel and joyless),* even if man desired it and could bring it about under the conditions of competition and economic and political difficulties. Various sides of scientific and technological progress—urbanization, industrialization, mechanization, automation, the use of fertilizers and chemical weed-killers, the growth of culture and leisure time, medical progress, better nourishment, the lowering of the mortality rate, and the prolonging of life—are closely interconnected, and *there is no possibility of "turning back" some aspects of progress without destroying all of civilization.*[5] (Emphasis added.)

Sakharov reiterated the point with even greater force in his Nobel lecture in 1975. Responding directly to Solzhenitsyn's proposals for the resuscitation of a traditional society, he argued that

any attempt to reduce the tempo of scientific and technological progress, to reverse the process of urbanization, to call for isolationism, patriarchal ways of life, and a renaissance based on ancient national traditions, would be unrealistic. Progress is indispensable, and *to halt it would lead to the decline and fall of our civilzation.*[6] (Emphasis added.)

Sakharov is careful to add that his version of progress also entails the development of humanistic values, which will emerge as a natural consequence of the rationalization of society. Indicting Solzhenitsyn for confusing progress with the mere growth of industry and technology, he argues that progress must also be measured in terms of the increasing ability of the nation to cope rationally with a growing set of social and environmental problems and to maintain an open society. "Progress must continuously and expediently change its concrete forms," he points out, meaning that it should be thought of as a process which includes not only technological adaptation to new physical realities but also the alteration of past notions of man's place in the physical and social order.[7] The end result is to be a subtle combination of the "scientific and democratic regulation of the world economy and social life"[8] and the emergence of a humanistic system of values in which the "moral factor" will emerge as a natural consequence of rationalization and serve as a guardian of "man's freedom of conscience and his moral yearning for the good."[9] It is clear that Sakharov's concern with technological advancement has not blinded him to the moral questions which are at the core of Solzhenitsyn's writings; quite to the contrary, Sakharov sees the sense of moral rebirth which Solzhenitsyn seeks as inseparably linked to his concern about the modernization of Russia. The difference between the two men is not *whether* moral standards of conduct are to emerge as an important part of the definition of man's place in the social and technological order, but whether they would emerge from a presumably integrated traditional culture or from a rationalized social order.

The rational control of further progress is also seen as dependent upon certain "intellectual factors"—Sakharov clearly has in mind leadership of the scientific community as a guiding if not directly governing force—which are characteristically "underestimated" in the socialist countries, due to the "populist-ideological dogmas of official philosophy."[10]

Again there is the subtle mixture of elitist and democratic elements, as in his early formulation of the "scientific *and* democratic regulation" of economic and social life. Citing the public discussion of environmental problems as an example of such combined action between the scientific elite and informed public opinion, Sakharov observes that the "partial liberalization in our country after the death of Stalin made it possible to engage in public debate on this problem during the 1960s,"[11] a freedom that has disappeared under the repressive hand of the current regime. Yet to avoid the "witting or unwitting abuse of progress," it is necessary to possess "freedom of conscience, the existence of an informed public opinion, a pluralistic system of education, freedom of the press, and access to other sources of information . . . ," all of which are "in short supply" in the socialist nations.[12]

Since he argues that many of the desirable manifestations of a rationalized society are already present in the more mature and technologically advanced states of the West, Sakharov is critical of Solzhenitsyn's denunciation of the penetration of allegedly pernicious Western ideas and his call for a distinctly Russian path of development. For Sakharov, the distinctions between East and West are clearly less significant than those separating mature industrial systems from their more primitive Soviet and East European counterparts. The goal ought not to be to isolate Russia from the further influence of Western technology and to glorify distinctive patterns of development:

Likewise, I do not share Solzhenitsyn's view of the role of Marxism as a supposedly "Western" and anti-religious doctrine which has distorted the healthy Russian pattern of development. The very division of ideas into Western and Russian is incomprehensible to me. In a scientific, rational approach to social and natural phenomena, ideas and concepts are divided into true ones and fallacious ones. *And where is that healthy Russian pattern of development? Has there really been even one moment in the history of Russia, or in any country for that matter, when it was capable of developing without contradictions and cataclysms?*[13] (Emphasis added.)

Reversing the argument, Sakharov says that no one nation can hope to meet both the social and technological challenges of the latter half of the twentieth century without assistance from others. "The salvation of our country," says Sakharov, employing the same word earlier used by Solzhenitsyn for the revival of their homeland "—in its interdependence with all the rest of the world—is impossible without saving all of humanity."[14]

He concludes:

Only on a global scale is it possible to solve the scientific-technical problems of our time such as the creation of nuclear and thermo-nuclear energetics, a new agricultural technology, the production of synthetic substitutes for albumin, the problem of building cities, the construction of an industrial technology that will not defile the environment, the mastery of space, the fight against cancer and cardiovascular diseases, the development of cybernetic technology. These tasks require outlays of many billions of dollars, which are beyond the scope of any individual state.[15]

This mutual dependence will have a marked effect on political and social developments within the USSR itself, a fact that is important in Sakharov's hope for gradual reform:

Our country cannot live in economic and scientific-technical isolation without world trade, including trade in the nation's resources, and detached from world progress. *Rapprochement with the West must have the character of the first stage of a convergence and be accompanied by democratic reforms in the USSR, partly self-initiated and partly prompted by economic and political pressure from abroad. . . . Then it will become impossible to retain other antidemocratic institutions in the country; it will be necessary to bring living standards into line with those in the West, and there will be a free exchange of people and ideas.*[16] (Emphasis added.)

Given this frame of reference, it is understandable that Sakharov is skeptical of Solzhenitsyn's appeals to Russian nationalism or to the "special suffering" of the Russian people as justifications for breaking with the West and insuring the survival of the nation through the exclusive development of the Northeast. While he acknowledges the natural tendency to stress the unique burdens of one's own people, he terms it an "appeal to patriotism . . . straight out of the arsenal of semi-official propaganda."[17] Sakharov argues instead that the most traumatic social and political dislocations of the twentieth century are not uniquely Russian but have beset all major industrial nations. Even granting Solzhenitsyn the benefit of the doubt concerning the nonaggressive intentions of his sense of Russian nationalism, Sakharov cautions against the perversion of an otherwise benign doctrine:

It may be said that Solzhenitsyn's nationalism is not aggressive; that it is of a mild, defensive character and aims to save and restore our long-suffering nation. *But we know from history that the "ideologues" were always milder than the practical politicians who came after them.* Among much of the Russian people and many of the nation's leaders there exist sentiments of Great Russian nationalism combined with a fear of becoming dependent upon the West, and a fear of democratic reforms. *Falling on such fertile soil, Solzhenitsyn's mistakes may become dangerous.*[18] (Emphasis added.)

On the question of developing the Northeast, Sakharov calls for cooperative international measures to tap the region's plentiful natural resources, which are then to be utilized for the benefit of all mankind.[19] Arguing that Solzhenitsyn has "exaggerated the role of industrial gigantism in the development of the difficulties of the modern world," Sakharov cautions that deconcentrating industry into smaller units would encounter technical, social, demographic, and even climatic problems of monumental proportions. He bitterly condemns the proposal to create small-scale industrial settlements in the Northeast:

The commune does not seem to me a panacea for all ills [of industrial and urban society], although I do not deny its attractiveness under certain conditions. Solzhenitsyn's dream of the possibility of getting along with the simplest kind of equipment, almost manual labor, appears impractical and foredoomed to failure under the difficult conditions of the Northeast. *His program is more myth-making than a real project. But the creation of myth is not always a harmless thing, especially in the twentieth century;* we yearn for them. The myth of a "reservoir" for the Russian nation may turn into a tragedy.[20] (Emphasis added.)

Sakharov also questions Solzhenitsyn's assertion that the most salient characteristic of the present Soviet leaders is their devotion to Marxism-Leninism. He rejects the entire notion that ideology per se can be the principal mainspring of modern society and argues that Solzhenitsyn's belief that all would be well if a "correct" ideology governed society creates potential dangers. He charges that Solzhenitsyn

overstates the ideological factor in contemporary Soviet society. *Hence the belief that the replacement of Marxism by a healthy ideology*—and he apparently sees Orthodoxy in this role—*will save the Russian people.* This belief underlies his whole conception. *But I am convinced that the nationalist and isolationist trend of*

*Solzhenitsyn's thinking, and his special brand of religious-pa-
triarchal romanticism, are leading him toward substantial mistakes, and make his proposals utopian and potentially dangerous.*[21]
(Emphasis added.)

Despite his differing assessment of the importance of ideology,
Sakharov joins with Solzhenitsyn in calling upon Soviet leaders
to renounce Marxism as an official creed. But while Solzhenitsyn
bases this recommendation on his view that Marxism-Leninism
is inherently a foreign doctrine, Sakharov reaches the same substantive conclusion through reasoning that official doctrine has
been an obstacle to material and technical progress and has therefore retarded the adaptation of Soviet society to the "second industrial revolution." What bothers Sakharov is not that Marxism
is essentially materialistic in focus, but rather that it has been
applied in a crude and inflexible manner to justify the investment
of considerable national energies in the support of dubious worldwide projects and the maintenance of a technologically backward
economy. Thus it has become what he would term an anti-pro-
gressive force, although he does argue that much of the visible
overlay of ideology in Soviet life is merely a convenient facade
behind which Soviet leaders conceal their essentially self-serving
efforts to resist any change that would diminish the jealously guarded
powers of the party.[22]

In terms of identifying the "carriers" of this new sense of progress and modernity, Sakharov's writings offer us an ambiguous
and seemingly contradictory set of assumptions. The ambiguity
is perhaps best seen in his call for the "scientific and democratic
regulation of the world economy and social life," which mixes
elements of technocratic elitism and democratic egalitarianism.[23]
In his own mind, Sakharov seems to accept the argument that,
in the long run, there is no necessary contradiction between the
notion of a planned society heavily dependent upon its technocratic elite and the concept of democratic rule, although he does
provide for a gradual transition period to shift from the present
autocratic system to democratic institutions.

Sakharov strongly implies that he sees the scientific and technical
intelligentsia as the principal "carriers" of the concept of "progress"

and as the primary movers in the process of rationalizing society. Working within a much looser and more pluralistic institutional and political structure than that envisioned by Solzhenitsyn, they will act as the catalysts of social and economic change and provide the necessary expertise for the further development of society. While they will enjoy preeminent status in a society in which one's place within the pecking order is determined by the "type of occupation" and the "nature of [one's] abilities," they will work within a competitive political structure which encourages rational discussion and free inquiry into the nature of social problems.[24] What is distinctive about their role is not their possession of some "truth" defined in cultural or ideological terms, but rather their mastery of functionally necessary skills and their devotion to a limitless and highly individualistic search for the rational social order. Clearly implicit in Sakharov's thinking about the role of these social forces as "carriers" is the notion that ultimately the same understanding of what "rationality" and "progress" mean in practical terms will be shared by the average citizen, who, while not possessing the highly developed skills of the technocrats, will nonetheless be capable of comprehending the basic direction of social development and accepting the leading role of the intelligentsia.

SOCIAL AND POLITICAL CHANGE

For Sakharov, the driving forces behind the social and political transformation of all industrial societies are found in what he has termed "techno-economic progress." As a result of technical and economic imperatives, all industrial nations have come to share a common set of problems and to be confronted with roughly similar patterns of social transformation, although the overlay of tradition and authoritarian rule in the USSR may retard the emergence of elements common to all. Borrowing a term also used by Western commentators, Sakharov describes this as a process of convergence, which will ultimately lead to a new social order combining elements of the present capitalist and socialist systems.[25]

In Sakharov's mind, the process of convergence entails not only a conscious technological and sociological restructuring of society, but also the creation of democratic political institutions and the recognition of a new standard of humanistic values. Thus material-technical progress, democratization, and the protection of individual freedoms are viewed as mutually interdependent; humanistic values are seen as a necessary condition for the functioning of an open and rationalized society, and it is in such a social setting that they can best be realized and defended. Convergence is also seen as a key to reducing the level of conflict within and among nations, and the recognition of the world's "true" problems—the need for scientific progress and rationally planned social action—will dwarf less relevant concerns of class conflict and national rivalries. Sakharov thus presents an optimistic picture of a world in which such convergence occurs: "The convergence of the Socialist and capitalist systems would be accompanied by demilitarization, the strengthening of international trust, and the defense of human rights, law, and freedom. Profound social progress and democratization would follow, and man's moral, spiritual, and personal resources would be strengthened."[26]

For Sakharov, convergence is both a social and technological progress which has already begun, albeit with greater effect in the West, and a program for positive reform against which the actions of the Soviet government are to be measured. His first writings on the topic were contained in his 1968 essay *Progress, Coexistence, and Intellectual Freedom* and expressed a now admittedly overly optimistic view of the pace and salutary consequence of convergence. In the 1968 essay, he detailed a four-stage process of change to be followed by the USSR and Western industrial nations.[27] Stage one, which began approximately in 1960 and extended until 1980, was to be characterized by a growing ideological struggle within the socialist countries between antiprogressive "Stalinist-Maoist" forces and the "realistic forces of leftist Leninist Communists" (read: moderate reformers).[28] This was to lead to the development of a deep ideological split at the national, international, and intraparty levels and the possible emergence of a multiparty system within socialist countries, although the latter is not essential for convergence to continue. What is essential is the eventual victory of the moderate reform wing of the party, which will in turn lead to continued economic reforms, the strengthening of democracy, the protection of individual rights, and continued peaceful coexistence with other social systems.[29]

The focus of stage two shifts to the West and is marked by the victory of the "leftist reformist wing of the bourgeoisie," or in less arcane language, of the moderate, nondogmatic Western reformers who also accept the notion of convergence. Spurred on by demands for social progress and peaceful coexistence, they undertake extensive social welfare programs, cooperation with the socialist nations on an international scale, and "changes in the structure of ownership" within the capitalist world. Sakharov describes this process as "a program of rapprochement (convergence) with socialism," demonstrating once again that he equates the two processes and that Western nations will eventually come to mirror more and more of the characteristics of socialism as convergence continues. During this phase, which will occur from 1972 through to 1985 according to the author's original timetable, there will be an "expanded role for the intelligentsia" in the Western nations, since Sakharov sees his Western counterparts as the obvious carriers of the sense of "progress" and social rationality in the capitalist world.[30]

The third stage will occur from 1972 to 1990 and be characterized both by the simultaneous disarmament of the two major powers and by the extension of technological and humanitarian assistance to the third world. Sakharov recommends that each nation annually give 20 percent of its gross national product to poorer nations so that they might proceed with industrialization. Even for the third world, Sakharov's solutions are heavily laced with an unquestioning reliance on technology. The whole purpose of extensive external assistance is to overcome the trap of poverty and to foster indigenous industrial growth.[31]

The fourth stage, from 1980 to the year 2000, is marked by the "socialist convergence" of the two systems which will "reduce differences in social structure, promote intellectual freedom, science, and economic progress, and lead to creation of a world government and the smoothing of national contradictions."[32] Viewing the ultimate "converged" society as a social and technological utopia, Sakharov cautions that the preservation of an open society will "require the greatest possible scientific foresight and care and concern for human values of a moral, ethical, and personal character. (I [have] touched briefly on the danger of a thoughtless bureaucratic use of the scientific and technological revolution in a divided world . . . but I could add a great deal more)."[33] He adds that these dangers can be avoided "only under highly intelligent worldwide guidance."[34]

Returning to the topic in 1972, Sakharov added the observation that the capitalist and the socialist systems will each have different obstacles to overcome during convergence. In the West, the primary political battles will be fought over the further assertion of "workers' rights" [read: the reduction of the political power of the business community and a more equitable distribution of wealth] and limitations on the military, while the most critical struggles in the Soviet Union will be fought over attempts "to reduce the militarization of the economy" and to lift the party monopoly over virtually every aspect of life. Sakharov also speaks of the need to limit the rule of a "messianic ideology," which brings him closer to Solzhenitsyn's assessment of the nature and importance of Marxism-Leninism to Soviet leaders.[35]

Sakharov has held firmly to his notion of convergence in spite of the increasing repression by Soviet authorities of virtually all elements of the reform movement. While he acknowledges that his original optimistic views about convergence were formed during the time of Dubček reforms in Czechoslovakia, he nonetheless maintains that the central core of his convergence theory remains unchanged. He admitted in June, 1972, that his earlier timetable had been overly optimistic—the Soviet-led invasion of Czechoslovakia and increasingly severe repression at home had obviously taken their toll—but he reasserted in August, 1973, that the "basic premises" of the 1968 argument still were valid.[36] The only complicating factor first introduced into the argument in 1973 was that continued American-Soviet détente might occur without the necessary democratization or loosening of political controls in the USSR, leaving it essentially a closed society unable to transform itself along the lines envisioned by the author.[37] By 1975, however, the whole issue of convergence had slipped to the level of a secondary concern in the author's writings, where it remains today. In his essay *My Country and the World*, Sakharov shifts the tone of his comments away from what he now refers to as "the dream" of convergence toward a concrete assessment of "the dangers, illusions, and dramas of today: everything that stands between the dream and reality."[38] He speaks in far more pessimistic tones than ever before about the retarded development of his homeland and the increasing repressiveness of its institutions. Expressing his fear that the West too has drifted away from the path of convergence because it has experienced a loss of its sense of a moral purpose and humanism and a failure of will vis-à-vis the Soviet Union—charges similar in tone if not in intensity to Solzhenitsyn's indictment—he stops short of recanting his view that convergence remains a long-term *goal* even though the immediate *process* has fallen on hard times.[39]

By 1977, his assessment of, if not his ultimate hopes for, convergence had grown even more pessimistic. Now even more seriously doubting that the Soviet system is capable of "independent, harmonious, and gradual development within its own frontiers," Sakharov concludes that he is "less certain of the reciprocal evolution of totalitarian socialism toward pluralism."[40] Such evolution will depend upon overcoming the closed nature of the society, a development that Sakharov also views as unlikely, since the Soviet system "apparently requires expansion, informational isolation, and demagogic self-praise" if it is to survive.[41]

In spite of his earlier reservations, Sakharov still offers a far more sanguine view of the West's prospects for evolutionary change toward his version of "socialist" convergence. "Today's capitalist society," he argues, "with a few reservations, can be called 'capitalism with a human face.' "[42] Crediting this development both to "the great achievements of science and engineering" in creating sufficient material well-being to alleviate the dilemma of the distribution of wealth, and to the "ideas of social justice, human rights, and democracy which have permeated social consciousness" as a consequence both of Christianity and other religious doctrines and of a century and a half of socialist thought, including Marxism, Sakharov concludes that socialist ideas, in their pluralistic antitotalitarian form will continue to play a definite role in Western social development. This will in fact be the movement of the West toward convergence with the socialist world.[43] In fostering this evolution, a significant role will be played by the increasingly popular and parliament-oriented Western communist parties, which "have been moving away from pro-Soviet dogmatism toward classical social-democratic ideology."[44]

Since Sakharov views the process of Soviet-American détente as inextricably linked to the prospects for liberalization within the USSR itself, he has tried to maintain a careful distinction between the continuing need for a mutually beneficial relationship between the two superpowers on the one hand, and a realistic assessment of Soviet goals and an appreciation of the dangers—both to the West and for the evolution of Soviet political life as well—if détente is perverted into an unprincipled desire for improved relations at any cost. He is unambiguous in asserting the positive value of détente in terms of exerting pressure on Soviet leaders:

We must not forget that only détente created the possibility of exerting even minimal influence on both the domestic and foreign policies of the Socialist countries. In the name of détente, they are required to accommodate their actions to universal humanitarian standards. It would be a great misfortune to return to the past.[45]

Moreover, détente is also viewed as a *sine qua non* of meaningful disarmament efforts, although Sakharov is skeptical of the firm resolve of some Western leaders to resist the temptation to exploit "transitory political situations at home" favoring quick treaty commitments and to insist upon the maintenance of "equal strength."[46]

On the other hand, Sakharov warns of the seductive behavior of Soviet leaders, who, having "encountered substantial difficulties both in domestic development and in relations with the outside world . . . have been finally forced to modify their tactics and appearances, although without initial changes in the system's ultimate goals."[47] While he personally believes that such tactical shifts have "brought on important changes at deeper levels," Sakharov nonetheless cautions against two potential extremes in the Western response to the USSR. Echoing Solzhenitsyn, he warns that "on the international level, one danger is the loss of Western unity and of a clear understanding of the ever-constant global threat posed by totalitarian nations. The West must not under any circumstances allow the weakening of its own stand against totalitarianism."[48] In one of its several guises, détente is thus seen as "camouflage" which masks both continuing Soviet expansionism and increasingly severe repression at home, while seductively luring the West into a state of disunity and inaction. Yet at the other extreme, he also cautions against the reverse assumption that both Soviet economic and military power—the alleged might of both being seriously undercut by technological inadequacies, according to Sakharov—are sufficient to require concessions from the West. Such actions would only postpone "the evil day" of confrontation and reckoning and create "another version of Munich."[49]

Sakharov predictably supports Western attempts to influence the treatment of Soviet dissidents, although he has grown increasingly skeptical of the Carter administration's once touted attention to such matters. Terming the defense of such rights as "an essential foundation of the pursuit of international stability and confidence," he chides both Western politicians who persist in "short-sighted pragmatism" and critics anywhere who charge that Western criticism impedes disarmament talks. He reasons that since any lasting and meaningful commitment to disarmament must also include the creation of an open and pluralistic society within the USSR, the issue of human rights is central to the achievement of arms limitations measures. In the short run, he recommends partial boycotts or cutoffs of scientific and cultural exchanges and certain types of technology, but the trade of foodstuffs is to remain insulated from such political considerations. Arms limitations talks are to be similarly set aside from other considerations and to be continued without preconditions.[50]

Returning to the domestic issue of the social structure of all advanced industrial nations, Sakharov took note in his 1968 memorandum of the emergence both of the scientific and technocratic intelligensia and of a separate managerial class. Speaking of the latter, he observed that "the development of modern society in both the Soviet Union and the United States is now following the same course of increasing complexity of structure and of industrial management, *giving rise in both countries to managerial groups that are similar in social character.*"[51] (Emphasis added.) Sakharov quickly adds, however, that the closed nature of Soviet society retards the further development of these strata as well as the self-recognition of their role in a future society. But in theory, stratification in such a society is to be based on the "type of occupation" and the "nature of abilities," suggesting that at least in his earliest writings Sakharov had a sort of technocratic and managerial meritocracy in mind.[52] The only other social group to receive specific recognition in Sakharov's scheme of things is simply termed "the working class," which is described as capable of sharing the author's devotion to "progress" and social rationalization, although it is only gradually to be involved in the business of government.[53] Fearful of the possibility that the working class may be misled, especially in the initial phases of democratization, Sakharov warns of the manipulation of a politically less sophisticated society through mass psychology and even biochemical means; moreover, like Solzhenitsyn, he indicts the phenomenon of mass culture as antithetical to human freedom and the development of a rational world view.[54]

Concerning the political institutions of a fully "converged" Soviet society, Sakharov seems initially to differ with Solzhenitsyn on the question of democratization. Noting that in his *Letter to the Soviet Leaders*, Solzhenitsyn had expressed doubts about the prospects for democracy in the USSR, Sakharov offers the view that

these opinions are alien to me. *I consider the democratic path to be the only possible one for any country.* The servile, slavish spirit which existed in Russia for centuries, combined with a scorn for people of other countries, other races, and other beliefs, was in my view the greatest of misfortunes. *Only under democratic conditions can one develop a national character capable of intelligent existence in a world becoming increasingly complex. Of course there is a kind of vicious circle here which cannot be overcome in a short time.*[55] (Emphasis added.)

The last sentence provides an enlightening clue to Sakharov's real understanding of the democratic process. Like Solzhenitsyn, he is at heart an antirevolutionary figure, a moderate and self-confessed "gradualist" hopeful of controlled political change that would shift power from the existing political elite into the hands of the managerial and technocratic groups which will come to dominate a "converged" society. In a memorandum written jointly with V. F. Turchin and Roy A. Medvedev in 1970, Sakharov explicitly spells out the dangers inherent in too rapid a process of democratization, including the survival of "individualist, antisocial forces," "worshipers of strong power, demagogues of a fascist type," the "mistrust" that might emerge between the party apparatus and the nonparty intelligentsia, into whose hands power would gradually shift, and still-surviving "bourgeois and nationalist sentiments" among the population at large.[56] Taken together, this list of possible calumnies reveals an apprehension that the process of change might escape rational control and give rise to a demagogic political style even less well-suited to the emergence of Sakharov's rationalized social order. Thus in their original commentary on the pace of reforms, Sakharov and his coauthors called in 1970 for "democratization at the initiative of, and under the control of, the highest authorities, [that] will allow this process to advance gradually and thus to enable all the links of the Party-state apparatus successfully to change over to the new style of work."[57] Even the dissemination of accurate information about the present state of the nation and the economy is to be restricted at the beginning of the transition period, and the circle of those included in such frank discussions will be gradually enlarged to include wider segments of the society as rationalization continues (although repression of all dissidents is to be ended immediately and complete amnesty for political prisoners offered).[58]

Viewing the increasing repression in his homeland, Sakharov has grown increasingly skeptical about the prospects for reform initiated from above, although he still describes himself as a gradualist.[59] He is now considerably less sanguine about the likelihood that would-be reformers within the present leadership—the people whom he termed the "leftist Leninist Communists" in 1968—either desire or are capable of undertaking reforms. By 1975, in his essay *My Country and the World*, he shifted tone and described the party in monolithic terms as simply a "monopoly" of all political and economic power. Speaking of the "conservatism, cowardice, and selfish interests of the *nomenklatura* [that is, the top office holders in the party and state hierarchies],"[60] Sakharov suggested that he now views the Communist Party as a totally stagnant and regressive force motivated by self-interest and the desire to preserve the prerogatives of power; he goes so far as to argue that membership in the top echelons has become virtually "hereditary," passing from generation to generation because of the obvious educational and social advantages possessed by the sons and daughters of the elite.[61] His characterization of the regime has also hardened considerably; both in the essay *My Country and the World* and in the Nobel lecture in 1975, he referred to it as "totalitarian," adding the highly critical epithet of "state capitalism" in the former.[62]

Sakharov's pessimism concerning the basic health of Soviet society has also deepened in recent years. Lamenting the loss of the "great hopes, efforts to increase productivity, [and] a spirit of dedication and sacrifice" that marked the first years of the fledging Soviet regime, Sakharov now argues that

a deeply cynical caste society has come into being, one which I consider dangerous (to itself as well as to all mankind)—a sick society ruled by two principles: *blat* (a little slang word meaning, "You scratch my back and I'll scratch yours"), and the popular saw: "No use banging your head against the wall."[63]

In such a setting, careerism and petty corruption abound at all levels, breeding a deep distrust of the institutions of party and state which tolerate—and some would say depend upon—such behavior and resulting in the "debasement and corruption of millions of people" whose lives have become twentieth-century incarnations of the parodies of Chekhov or Gogol.

A similar reconsideration can be seen in the author's political self-definition. Writing in *Progress, Coexistence, and Intellectual Freedom* in 1968, Sakharov was unabashedly prosocialist in terms of lauding the positive social reforms of his nation and the eventual "socialist" convergence of the major industrial states. This optimism was also clearly reflected in his call for party-led reforms in the 1970 essay coauthored with Turchin and Medvedev, although those elements of the study may have been more reflective of the latter's thinking at the time. By December, 1972, in an interview with a Western reporter, he seems to reverse himself, saying that "I would no longer label myself a socialist. I am not a Marxist-Leninist, a Communist. I would call myself a liberal."[64] But by 1975, Sakharov seems once again to have returned to the fold, albeit both wistfully and skeptically; in *My Country and the World*, he once again refers to "basically sound socialist ideas"[65] which have been distorted by both the Russians and the Chinese, and confesses that

I believe that in principle "socialism with a human face" is possible, and represents a high form of social organization. But it is possible only as a result of extraordinary collective efforts, plus wisdom and selflessness exercised by a great part of the people. . . . The total nationalization of all means of production, the one-party system, and the repression of honest convictions—all this must be avoided or totalitarianism will prevail.[66]

Repeatedly in his references to the political life of modern society, Sakharov returns to the interlocking themes of democratization, an open society, institutional and philosophical pluralism, and the defense of human rights. Beginning with his 1968 essay *Peace, Coexistence, and Intellectual Freedom* and extending throughout all of his subsequent writings, he calls for the creation of democratic institutions, and the establishment of a multiparty system within his homeland,[67] for an active and independent role for professional and other voluntary associations in the political process (including the right to publish their own views unhampered by censorship),[68] and for the "basic aim" of government to be "the protection and safeguarding of the basic rights of its citizens."[69]

Against this must be weighed Sakharov's concern that the process of democratization occur only gradually and with careful safeguards—a transitory problem if we grant that the author may be concerned in this comment with the *pace* rather than the *end result* of reforms—and his initial and clearly elitist assumption that a benevolent strata of technocrats and managers will emerge to lead society once democratization has occurred. The key to

understanding the latter point is Sakharov's belief that the process of democratization will be more than a simple extension of an
effective franchise to the community as a whole. Rather it is seen
also as a process of *uplifting* and *transforming* the masses through
free, rational discussion of the alternatives until all agree on the
"rationality" and progressive nature of the sort of reforms Sakharov
has in mind. While "every honorable and thinking person . . . will
seek to insure that future development will be along the lines of
the better alternative [that is, convergence and modernization as
opposed to technical and cultural regression]," it will be necessary
to use "broad, open discussion, without the pressure of fear and
prejudice . . . [to] *help the majority to adopt the correct and best
course of action.*"[70] (Emphasis added.) Sakharov certainly does not
imply that differences of opinion will not arise, but, working within his frame of reference, he believes that such disputes can be
rationally settled since there is a "correct" solution which will
eventually be accepted by all participants. He reminds his readers
that among both leaders and the common people there exists "a
fear of democratic reforms,"[71] and cautions against any form of
"political struggle, which would inevitably incite people to violence,
sectarianism, and frenzy,"[72] or, in other words, lead them to
behave in nonrational (not irrational) ways. Translated into the
jargon of Western students of decision making, Sakharov clearly
views the political process as essentially an exercise in problem
solving in which all participants possess the same perceptions and
values, permitting a single, commonly accepted and rationally
"correct" decision to emerge once all the factors have been weighed,
in contrast to a much looser process in which bargaining and
adjustment must occur to balance the interests of dissimilar participants who do not share the same aspirations or frames of
reference.[73] At no time does Sakharov describe his conception
of the political process as anything other than a planning process;
the pluralists' understanding of the politics as a give-and-take
battle defined by and contained within procedural guidelines is
totally absent. But as any Western student of the planning process
can quickly demonstrate (and as Soviet experience also indicates),
the search for a rational plan, even when goals are held in common,
rapidly deteriorates into a highly partisan confrontation when

allocations and organizational prerogatives are at stake. It must also be recalled that Sakharov has never spoken of direct popular participation in the process of making public policy, but rather merely of ultimate "accountability,"[74] which is never defined in concrete institutional terms. It seems at least reasonable to argue, therefore, given Sakharov's repeated calls for the passage of various legislative acts to initiate reforms, he is content, at least in the beginning, to accept the basic soviet form of government so long as it operates openly and freely. He assumes, as did Solzhenitsyn, that it will ultimately reflect his priorities, in this case because of the compelling logic of a rational social order.

Sakharov's idea of the meaning of individual freedom also clearly reflects this basic orientation. He goes much further than Solzhenitsyn to assert a "pure" concept of freedom stripped of cultural restraints; an authoritarian system, even if rooted in tradition and culture, is unacceptable to him because it restricts the development of modern society. But one nonetheless senses in Sakharov's writings the assumption that his operational definition of freedom equates it with rational thought; that is, a free person is free to act rationally to find the best solution to the problems that beset his society. This interpretation is in keeping with the author's statement that the processes of democratization, scientific and technological progress, and convergence, all of which are seen as integral parts of rationalization, occur simultaneously and are mutually interdependent and supportive, and it is consistent with his tutorial approach to gradual democratization and the preparation of the public to play a greater role, however institutionally defined, in the affairs of government.

The leadership role which Sakharov envisions for the scientific-technical and managerial elites is also revealing of his understanding of what democracy will mean in practice. It has already been noted that the author accepts the argument that these social elements become increasingly important as the processes of modernization and convergence advance simply because they possess the skills needed to run an increasingly complex social and economic order. To this must be added his conviction not only that the technocrats and the managers are the people most capable of the rational consideration of alternatives, but also that the vast majority of the working class itself will recognize its common interests with the intelligentsia and accept its leadership.[75] Even though he later spoke out in his Nobel lecture against overly simplistic "technocratic options" for political and social reforms which stressed only the "material" and not the moral and humanistic aspects of man's existence, Sakharov has continued to stress the important role of these elements in modern society.[76] However, their actual political role has never been clearly defined, although it is probably safe to assume that, of necessity, they will occupy the upper echelons of industry and government. In addition, they are to be given a further role, through the creation of independent councils of scientists and technicians, of advising national leaders.[77] Even permitting a degree of institutional pluralism and healthy competition within this structure, it is clear that considerable power will remain in the hands of the technocratic and managerial elite simply because of the critical importance of planning in modern society. "It is also clear that it [rational political reform] must be supplemented by a plan for economic and social measures worked out by specialists. *We emphasize that democratization itself does not solve economic problems. It only creates the preconditions for their solution.*"[78] (Emphasis added.)

Beginning with his Nobel lecture in 1975, and with increasing force in his subsequent publications and public commentaries, Sakharov has placed growing emphasis on the importance of pluralism in modern society. While the inclusion of such pluralist commentary is entirely consistent with his earlier writings on the need for an open society, the evolution of Sakharov's views suggests that he is now sanctioning more than merely ideological or philosophical pluralism and has begun instead to speak of meaningful political pluralism within which political power is distributed among various presumably well organized elements of the society. He lauds the American trade union movement as a prime example of the sort of pluralism responsible for "the enormous, real power of your society, the profound source of its successes," and thus implies that this might be the genre of pluralism that he hopes to see emerge within his nation.[79] Unfortunately, however, he has not explored the further implications of the relationship between effective political pluralism on the one hand and the professed need for centralized, "rational" planning on the other.

There is also considerable ambiguity in Sakharov's thinking

about the nature of the multiparty system which he repeatedly advocates. Writing in 1975 in *My Country and the World*, he listed the creation of a multiparty system as a high priority reform but offered no explanation of the political function or social basis of such organizations. While it is easy to visualize such parties competing for representation in freely elected soviets, it is much more difficult to comprehend the ideological principles or social groups around which they might coalesce. Since he has argued that considerations of nationality or ethnicity are of little consequence in a modern society, Sakharov surely cannot view such parties as representing these interests except perhaps on a marginal basis. The representation of territorial entities per se is also not a promising prospect; Sakharov has argued that the kinds of problems which confront modern society transcend traditional geographic boundaries and do not lend themselves substantively to rational debate based on the principle of representing one region or district against another. It is perhaps more likely that Sakharov sees differing ideologies or points of view as one of the principal touchstones of party identity. He does argue for completely free discussion and the testing of ideas in a public forum, and he maintains that the proper tutorial role of the intelligentsia is to help the people to understand "the better alternative."[80] It is clear that he does not wish to see the political process become the testing ground for the frenzied battles of private interests not bound by the process of rational discussion. Given all of this, one feasible interpretation is that Sakharov envisions parties as essentially polite protagonists engaged in an on-going and loosely structured public debate both within the halls of government and in the society as a whole, with each of the participants exercising a high degree of self-restraint to keep within the limits of rational debate and sharing the same notions about general social goals and what constitutes the legitimate exercise of state power. Another equally viable and not necessarily contradictory interpretation would link such parties to occupational or functional interests. Given Sakharov's assumption that the future society will be stratified according to occupations, it is highly likely that identifiable social strata also would coalesce into politically relevant associations and play an active role in public affairs, either through the elected institutions or through the councils of experts. But since Sakharov never offers any distinction between the notion of a "political party" and our concept of an "interest group," a more precise understanding of how he sees the role of occupational and professional groupings is virtually impossible.

Ultimately, Sakharov foresees the emergence of a vaguely defined world government. While its institutional structure is never discussed by the author, it is clear that Sakharov expects that it too will be dominated by the same managerial and technocratic elements which will come to the fore in the mature industrial nations. Thus an especially heavy burden for creating such a government falls on the United States and the Soviet Union as the most advanced world powers, both in terms of their responsibilities for diminishing the level of international tension and in terms of providing the necessary leadership and skills.[81]

THE FUTURE SOCIETY

While the social and political structure of Sakharov's ideal society have already been discussed, consideration must also be given to additional elements of his thinking about the nature of the future which stress man's increasingly sophisticated technological ability to manipulate both nature and the lifestyle of mankind. In his earlier works such as *Progress, Coexistence, and Intellectual Freedom* and in an essay written in 1974 for the *Saturday Review: World* entitled "Tomorrow: The View from Red Square," Sakharov offers a clearly optimistic view of the future based on man's increasing scientific capability and his rational capacity to alter what he would term inappropriate or regressive political and social institutions. By the mid 1970s, the tone of his comments had shifted away from this self-confessed "optimistic futurology" to an examination of the further deterioration of the prospects for reform in his homeland, although he notes that "I have not basically changed the views which I formulated at that time" (in *Progress, Coexistence, and Intellectual Freedom*).[82] He repeated his "very close affinities" with thoughts expressed in the 1968 memorandum again in his Nobel lecture in 1975 and has continued to reiterate his commitment to the importance of further advances in medicine, energy development, agriculture, and space exploration.[83]

In his earlier works, Sakharov presents a number of "futurological hypotheses . . . of a scientific and technological character."[84] His most sweeping vision of the future is presented in the *Saturday Review: World* essay, in which he paints a picture of the physical structure of future human habitation:

I imagine a gradual (completed long after 2024) growth of two types of territory out of the industrial world that is overcrowded and inhospitable to human life and nature. I will conditionally term them "Work Territory" (WT) and "Preserve Territory" (PT). The PT, larger in area, will be set aside for maintaining the earth's ecological balance, for leisure activities, and for man to actively reestablish his own natural balance. The smaller and densely populated WT will be the area where people will spend most of their time.[85]

The industrial infrastructure and the nature of urban settlement within the Work Territories are described in terms that suggest a combination of highly automated and technologically manipulated work and living environments and a sufficient level of "conveniences and comforts of modern living" to permit the man of the future to pursue cultural and intellectual goals:

The WT will have intensive agriculture, nature will have been transformed completely to serve practical needs. All industry will be concentrated in giant automated and semi-automated factories. Almost all people will live in "super-cities," the centers of which will contain multi-storied apartment buildings with artificially controlled climate and lighting, with automated kitchens, landscape walls, and so on.

A large part of the cities will be made up of suburbs. . . I envisage those suburbs in terms of the suburbs of today's most comfortable countries: built up with small houses or cottages, with yards and gardens, children's organizations, sports fields, and swimming pools. They will have all of the conveniences and comforts of modern urban living, silent and comfortable public transportation, clean air, arts and crafts, and a free and varied cultural life.[86]

In a revealing comparison, Sakharov admits that he is patterning this image after "the life of a person from the middle class of our present-day developed countries," which is to serve as a standard for others to emulate.[87]

The Preserve Territories, on the other hand, will serve the dual purpose of preserving the world's ecological balance and of providing the residents of the Work Territories with an opportunity to escape their seemingly benevolent urban environment to reestablish their own "natural balance." Stressing the recuperative powers of such contact with nature, Sakharov continues,

the man of the future will have an opportunity, I hope, to spend a part, even though it will be the smaller part, of his time *in the more natural surroundings of the PT*. I predict that people will lead lives with a real social aim in the PT as well. *They will not only rest but also work with their hands and their heads, read, and think. They will live in tents or in houses they have built themselves, the way their ancestors did.*[88] (Emphasis added.)

Seen in this light, the PTs are strikingly close, both in physical character and in social and psychological significance, to the "new cities of the old type" which Solzhenitsyn wishes to see spring up in the Northeast. The principal difference is, of course, that Solzhenitsyn sees these settlements as the primary habitat of mankind and is willing to accept limitations on economic and technological development to preserve them, while Sakharov sees them in terms of convenient although obviously beneficial locations in which to strengthen man's comprehension of himself as a part of a larger environmental whole.

Projecting population growth rates into the future and allocating the earth's available land to productive utilization or Preserve Territories, Sakharov suggests that the area of the world's Work Territory will eventually comprise 30 million square kilometers, and its average population density will be 300 people per square kilometer. The Preserve Territories will include only 80 million square kilometers and support an average density of 25 people per square kilometer, with many of that number "on leave" from the Work Territories. Under these arrangements, the average person would be able to spend 20 percent of his or her time in a Preserve Territory. Additional productive territory will eventually be created in what Sakharov terms "flying cities"—artificial earth satellites which perform important and environmentally dangerous industrial functions—and by the creation of "subterranean cities for sleep and entertainment" below both Work and Preserve territories.[89]

Equally important as the restructuring of the world into Work and Preserve Territories is the impact that advanced technology will have on all aspects of life. Sakharov is unrestricted in his optimism about what technology can do for the man of the future. First taking up the question in *Progress, Coexistence, and Intellectual Freedom*, he predicts discoveries in biology and medicine that "will make possible effective control and direction of all life processes at the levels of the cell, organism, ecology, and society, from fertility and aging to psychic processes and heredity," and of similar advances in energy technology, electronics, cybernetics, transportation, communication, and space exploration, which "will require thousands of people to work and live continuously on other planets and on the moon, on artificial satellites and on asteroids whose orbits will have been changed by nuclear explosions."[90]

Such technological optimism is again reflected in his view of the future presented to the readers of the *Saturday Review: World*. He predicts a widespread changeover to "closed cycle" industrial processes to contain the growing threat of pollution and to recycle exhaustible natural resources, although he also adds that the production of snythetic materials will take pressure off potentially scarce natural products. As far as energy development is concerned, he predicts greater utilization of the nation's vast coal reserves (but with careful environmental safeguards) and increased reliance on nuclear and fusion power. In the area of transportation, the private automobile will be replaced by environmentally less threatening battery-powered vehicles or by devices that move on "mechanical legs that will not disturb the grass cover or require asphalt roads." For long distances, freight and passengers will be moved in "atomic powered helium dirigibles" or in high-speed atomic trains, and in the cities people will move about on moving sidewalks or in automated shuttle vehicles.[91]

In order to meet the growing world demand for food, the so-called green revolution in agriculture will be intensified, including not only the continued application of more sophisticated fertilizers (an area of environmental concern with which Sakharov does not agree) and the creation of "artificial superfertile soil." Ultimately, cultivation will be extended to presently unproductive land areas, including the Northeast, where hothouses, artificial sunlight, heated soil, and hydroponics will make year-round production possible. New forms of marine, bacterial, microalgal, and fungal agriculture will be developed, and the "surface of the oceans, of Antarctica, and, ultimately of the moon and the planets as well, will be gradually adapted for agricultural use."[92]

Sakharov also sees advanced technology as a source of an information and communications revolution with profound social and political implications. He foresees "far in the future" the creation of a "universal information system . . . which will give everyone access at any given moment to the contents of any book that has ever been published or any magazine or any fact" through worldwide computer storage and recall facilities. In the more immediate future, he foretells the development of a "single global telephone and videophone system" to facilitate communications across national boundaries. Taken together, both elements of the communications revolution are important parts of the rationalization of society and the emergence of a well-informed debate about the nature of future progress. It must be recalled that one of the author's most vigorous indictments of both the present regime and of Solzhenitsyn's call for cultural separatism is that the sort of isolation that they produce would cut the intelligentsia off from productive contacts with their counterparts in more advanced industrial nations and thus retard the modernization of Russia herself. Moreover, freedom of information is a necessary prerequisite for the rational discussion of social issues, which is itself a precondition for the emergence of Sakharov's concept of democracy. In addition, this information retrieval and communications network becomes an important link in carrying the message of modernization and democratization to the general population through promoting "intellectual and artistic development."[93] Scorning the superficiality of the current mass media, Sakharov concludes that "unlike television, the major source of information for many of our contemporaries, the UIS [universal information system] will give each person maximum freedom of choice and will require individual activity."[94]

NOTES

1. Andrei D. Sakharov, "Alarm and Hope," Nobel essay written in March, 1977, in Andrei D. Sakharov, *Alarm and Hope* (New York: Vintage, 1978), pp. 99–100.

2. Andrei D. Sakharov, "Peace, Progress and Human Rights: Nobel Peace Prize Lecture, 1975," in Sakharov, *Alarm and Hope*, p. 4.

3. Andrei D. Sakharov, *Progress, Coexistence, and Intellectual Freedom* (New York: Norton, 1968), p. 25; this work also appears in Harrison E. Salisbury, ed., *Sakharov Speaks* (New York: Vintage, 1974), pp. 15–114. Page references hereafter are to the 1968 edition.

4. Sakharov, *Progress*, p. 71; A. D. Sakharov, V. F. Turchin, and R. A. Medvedev, "Manifesto II" [Letter to L. I. Brezhnev et al., dated 19 March 1970], in Salisbury, *Sakharov Speaks*, pp. 118–19, 123–29. Note that in his introduction written at a later date, Sakharov remarks that his views have evolved since his collaboration with Turchin and Medvedev; A. D. Sakharov, "Memorandum" (dated 5 March 1971), in Salisbury, *Sakharov Speaks*, p. 139.

5. Andrei D. Sakharov, "Tomorrow: The View from Red Square," *Saturday Review: World*, 24 August 1974, p. 110.

6. Sakharov, "Peace, Progress, and Human Rights," p. 9.

7. Andrei D. Sakharov, "In Answer to Solzhenitsyn," *New York Review of Books*, 13 June 1974, p. 3.

8. Ibid.

9. Andrei D. Sakharov, "Postscript to Memorandum," (postscript dated June, 1972, to "Memorandum") in Salisbury, *Sakharov Speaks*, p. 153.

10. Sakharov, "Peace, Progress, and Human Rights," p. 9.

11. Ibid.

12. Ibid.

13. Sakharov, "In Answer to Solzhenitsyn," p. 3.

14. Andrei D. Sakharov, *My Country and the World* (New York: Vintage, 1975), p. 45.

15. Sakharov, "In Answer to Solzhenitsyn," p. 4.

16. Ibid. A detailed examination of attitudes toward détente is beyond the present focus of this work; the reader should consult Frederick C. Barghoorn, *Détente and the Democratic Movement in the USSR* (New York: Free Press, 1976).

17. Sakharov, "In Answer to Solzhenitsyn," pp. 4–5.

18. Ibid.

19. Ibid., p. 3.

20. Ibid., p. 4.

21. Ibid.

22. Sakharov, *My Country*, pp. 30–31.

23. Sakharov, "In Answer to Solzhenitsyn," p. 3.

24. Sakharov, "Memorandum," p. 143.

25. For a general discussion of the Soviet debate over convergence, *see* Donald R. Kelley, "The Soviet Debate on the Convergence of the American and Soviet Systems," *Polity* 6, no. 2 (Winter, 1973), pp. 174–96.

26. Sakharov, "Tomorrow," p. 13.

27. Sakharov, *Progress*, pp. 81–84.

28. Ibid., pp. 81–82.

29. Ibid.

30. Ibid., pp. 82–83.

31. Ibid., p. 83.

32. Ibid., p. 83–84.

33. Ibid., p. 84.

34. Ibid.

35. Sakharov, "Postscript," p. 153.

36. Andrei D. Sakharov, "Interview with Western Correspondents, 21 August 1973," in Salisbury, *Sakharov Speaks*, pp. 203–4.

37. Ibid.

38. Sakharov, *My Country*, p. 5.

39. Ibid. The relevant sections are "Soviet Society," pp. 11–50, and "The Liberal Intelligentsia and the West," pp. 85–98.

40. Sakharov, "Alarm and Hope," p. 103.

41. Ibid., p. 104.

42. Ibid., p. 103.

43. Ibid.

44. Ibid., p. 104.

45. A. D. Sakharov, *Newsweek* interview, 24 February 1977, in Sakharov, *Alarm and Hope*, pp. 25–26.

46. Sakharov, "Alarm and Hope," pp. 104–5.

47. Ibid., p. 104.

48. Sakharov, *My Country*, p. 114.

49. Sakharov, "Peace, Progress, and Human Rights," p. 10.

50. Sakharov, *Newsweek* interview, pp. 25–26.

51. Sakharov, *Progress*, p. 76.

52. Sakharov, "Memorandum," pp. 142–44.

53. Sakharov, *My Country*, p. 97.

54. Sakharov, *Progress*, p. 58.

55. Sakharov, "In Answer to Solzhenitsyn," p. 4.

56. Sakharov, Turchin, and Medvedev, "Manifesto II," pp. 126–27.

57. Ibid.

58. Ibid., pp. 127–29.

59. Andrei D. Sakharov, interview with Olle Stanholm, Swedish radio correspondent, 3 July 1973, in Salisbury, *Sakharov Speaks*, p. 175; Sakharov, *My Country*, p. 102.

60. Sakharov, *My Country*, p. 46.

61. Ibid., p. 25.

62. Ibid., pp. 14–16; and "Peace, Progress, and Human Rights," pp. 100–101.

63. Sakharov, "Peace, Progress, and Human Rights," pp. 100–101.

64. Andrei D. Sakharov, "Interview with Jay Axelbank of *Newsweek*, 26 October 1972," *Sunday Observer* (London), 3 December 1972.

65. Sakharov, *My Country*, p. 88.

66. Ibid., pp. 91–92.

67. Ibid., p. 102.

68. Sakharov, Turchin, and Medvedev, "Manifesto II," pp. 127–29.

69. Sakharov, "Memorandum," p. 142.

70. Sakharov, *Progress*, p. 85.

71. Sakharov, "In Answer to Solzhenitsyn," pp. 4–5.

72. Sakharov, Turchin, and Medvedev, "Manifesto II," p. 129.

73. Paul Diesing, "Socioeconomic Decisions," *Ethics* 69 (1958), reprinted in *The Making of Decisions*, eds. William J. Gore and J. W. Dyson (New York: Free Press, 1964), pp. 64–84; Paul Diesing, *Reason in Society: Five Types of Decisions and their Social Conditions* (Westport, Conn.: Greenwood Press, 1973). For an application of this frame of reference to the USSR, *see* Donald R. Kelley, "Toward a Model of Soviet Decision Making: A Research Note," *American Political Science Review* 68, no. 2 (June, 1974, pp. 601–7.

74. Sakharov, *My Country*, p. 101.

75. Sakharov, *Progress*, p. 30.

76. Sakharov, "Peace, Progress, and Human Rights," p. 5.

77. Sakharov, "Postscript," p. 157; and *My Country*, p. 104.

78. Sakharov, Turchin, and Medvedev, "Manifesto II," p. 129.

79. A. D. Sakharov, address prepared for the AFL-CIO and read in the author's absence on 28 November 1977, in Sakharov, *Alarm and Hope*, pp. 162–63.

80. Sakharov, *Progress*, p. 85.

81. Sakharov, *My Country*, pp. 104-9; and "Peace, Progress, and Human Rights," pp. 10-11.

82. Sakharov, *My Country*, pp. 104-9.

83. Sakharov, "Peace, Progress, and Human Rights," p. 5.

84. Sakharov, "Tomorrow," p. 13.

85. Ibid., pp. 13-14.

86. Ibid., p. 14.

87. Ibid.

88. Ibid.

89. Ibid.

90. Sakharov, *Progress*, pp. 83-84.

91. Sakharov, "Tomorrow," p. 108.

92. Ibid.

93. Ibid.

94. Ibid.

6

In the Larger Perspective: The Dialogue as Commentary on Industrial Society

The dialogue between Alexander Solzhenitsyn and Andrei Sakharov is a discussion within which there are several discernible, if overlapping, levels of meaning and significance. Most visibly, it has been a dialogue about the consequences of repression within their homeland and a gentle but deeply rooted debate about appropriate strategies to employ to counter such actions. Both writers reject the Stalinist past, seeing little or no saving grace in the *Vozhd*'s successful, if costly, programs to industrialize the nation. Both also fear the continued presence of Stalin's "heirs" and brood over the ominous prospects that the next regime may turn decisively to the right, in part out of frustration at the failure of reforms, and in part because it may be an innate response of an inherently authoritarian social order.

Both Solzhenitsyn and Sakharov also share the view that the dissident community has had a significant impact on their homeland. Even though now smaller in number than at any time since the Twentieth Party Congress and under increasingly heavy attack from the regime, the "movement" has successfully broken through the silence of the previous two decades to raise the question of human rights in the Soviet Union and has laid the groundwork for future dissident activities. Significantly, neither figure envisions the future of the dissident community in terms of the emergence of an active resistance movement seeking to overthrow the regime by force; to the contrary, both reject the precedent that frustrated reformers give way to disciplined revolutionaries and counsel their followers to seek peaceful change.

At the second level of meaning and significance is the question of the future of Russia both as a nation and a culture. On this point, the authors differ on many critical questions, converging principally—and most importantly—on two commonly held themes: the need for meaningful guarantees of human rights and free speech and the necessity of avoiding the "frenzy" of partisan politics. But in virtually all other areas, they differ in their perception of a desirable future and the legitimacy of social and political institutions. While these differences are too extensive to summarize once again at this point, they amount to no less than fundamentally distinct views of the nature of man as a rational being and the nature of the social and political institutions that he can build and maintain in the modern world. From opening premise to final conclusion, each author constructs, implicitly or explicitly, a *Weltanschauung* not only with relevance for future developments within the Soviet Union, but also with deep implications for the further evolution or perhaps the very survival of modern industrial society.

The third level of meaning and significance broadens the perspective of the dialogue to an examination of many of the issues and dilemmas that have arisen in virtually all modern industrial states. The exceptional attention that has necessarily been devoted to the question of repression in the Soviet context has obscured the fact that much of the substance of the dialogue is a reflection of parallel discussions elsewhere about the fate of modern industrial society. No matter how differently explained, celebrated, or lamented, the contemporary nature and the future of that society have been at the center of a prolonged debate among its critics, defenders, and a host of seers who purport to discern its fate. Many of the issues raised in those discussions about the nature of contemporary man, the desirability of progress and growth, the impact of technology, the survival and adaptation of value systems, and the nature of social and political institutions are also clearly at the root of the Solzhenitsyn-Sakharov dialogue.

THE SLAVOPHILE-WESTERNIZER DICHOTOMY

Russian history itself tempts us with a convenient and deceptively meaningful frame of reference within which to lodge the Solzhenitsyn-Sakharov dialogue. The prolonged debate in the latter half of the nineteenth century between the Slavophiles and the Westernizers does admittedly make an uncritical examination of the present discourse seem *déjà vu*.[1] Both dialogues did indeed raise similar questions: what is unique and worth saving in traditional Russian culture; what is a proper response to an increasingly menacing Western culture; and what social and poliltical institutions are appropriate to accomplish these goals? But to accept the seductive notion that Solzhenitsyn and Sakharov are simply contemporary incarnations of the Slavophiles and Westernizers of an earlier century is both to distort and simplify their own views and to miss significant differences in the social, political, and technological milieux which have framed the respective discussions.

Undoubtedly the most significant difference which affects all aspects of the contemporary dialogue is the dispersion of the modern industrial system throughout the world. When earlier Slavophiles and Westernizers debated the course of the neophyte industrial order that had been established in tsarist Russia, there were then only the European and American experiences upon which they could base their fears or hopes. To be sure, important differences appeared even within the European and American prototypes, but in general, they shared many common features, most importantly the impact of industrialization and urbanization on traditional cultures and lifestyles. What before the turn of the century had been a dichotomous confrontation between proponents and opponents of a coherent industrial order modeled after the sole available prototype has now fractured into a multifaceted discussion of the impact of industrialization and modernization in a host of different cultural and national milieux. As studies such as Frederic Fleron's *Technology and Communist Culture* clearly demonstrate, even among socialist nations, the impacts of similar technologies and industrial processes have been mediated by a variety of indigenous factors, suggesting a multitracked rather than a unilinear pattern of development. Even greater diversity is found in the examples offered by third- and fourth-world nations, which have shown a high degree of eclecticism in selecting their own patterns of development.

Each in his own way, Solzhenitsyn and Sakharov evidence a comprehension of the complexity of the situation. Neither can be clearly placed within the simplistic frame of reference offered by nineteenth-century Slavophiles and Westernizers. At first reading, Solzhenitsyn seems closest to the historical model of a Slavophile thinker. As Stephen Carter has pointed out, many of his views resemble both Slavophile notions and those of the more obscure "native soil" (*pochvennichestvo*) movement of roughly the same era; the historically unique Russian experience is glorified as the source of a coherent and integrated culture and value system, and the concept of rationality is discounted in favor of an empathic emersion in the values, mores, and historical role of one's native land.[2] Yet as Carter himself acknowledges, Solzhenitsyn's comprehension of the world, while a reflection of these earlier views, shows considerably greater sophistication. Despite his attention to what may be termed the "nativist" elements of his own culture, Solzhenitsyn has a clearly expressed concept of mankind per se as a universal and value-creating phenomenon. As he argued in his Nobel lecture, Solzhenitsyn sees individual national cultures as forming the component parts of the larger notion of humanity. While the particularistic systems of culture, values, and unique historical experiences constitute separate and discernible entities, they are yet a variation—but an all-important variation, which is at the core of Solzhenitsyn's criticism of the standardization of modern industrial society—of the larger world culture, which is itself viewed as manifesting both common elements of all the lesser cultures and as possessing a divinely inspired essence that transcends rational understanding. The argument emerges with a pluralistic and relativistic tone if carried through to its logical conclusion: each national culture, if maintained in its purity, is a legitimate component of the human experience.[3]

Unlike the original Slavophiles, Solzhenitsyn does not manifest an innate hostility to Western culture per se. To be sure, he is critical of what he regards as the excessive rationalization and cultural standardization that Western culture has come to imply and of unthinking attempts to transplant such culture to other lands, positions which are consistent with his comprehension of national culture as unique and *sui generis*. But, as Carter observes, he specifically defends Western culture against what he sees as a growing threat from China, suggesting that his distaste of the West is tempered by an even greater fear of the corrosive impact of the East. Even more significantly, since his exile to the West, Solzhenitsyn has spoken with increasing emphasis of the need for Western cultures to return to what were presumably lost values of community, morality, and strength of will to resist the communist threat. Even discounting the obvious political purposes the author has in mind, it is still important to note that his argument is now with the *perversion* of what he regards as a once acceptably coherent and positive Western culture—acceptable, that is, for the West, but not his homeland—rather than with the phenomenon of Western culture per se. Read in this light, Solzhenitsyn comes curiously close to a position of cultural relativism—the theory that indigenous national cultures are historically rooted in time and location and serve, if undistorted by outside influence, to convey acceptable values and lifestyles to those who live within their fold.[4]

A careful reading of Solzhenitsyn's comments on science and technology also reveals a fairly sophisticated, if rhetorically exaggerated, comprehension of the nature of industrial society and the sorts of remedies that can be realistically pursued near the end of the twentieth century. He is not hostile to science and technology per se but rather to the uncritical extension of the intellectual frame of reference engendered by each into the realm of cultural and moral life. One might aruge that his true enemy is "scientization" rather than science itself, that is, the assumption that the logic of science can be applied to all spheres of life to eliminate empathy, intuition, and revelation as sources of knowledge.

On the other side of the dialogue, Andrei Sakharov is also an inappropriate candidate for the title of a modern-day Westernizer. To be sure, he accepts the notions of progress and rationality and celebrates at least most of the achievements of the modern industrial world. But his is a qualified acceptance of the real consequences of technology in modern society. Even more clearly than Solzhenitsyn, he perceives the negative impact that technology has had upon society as well as the moral dilemmas of further advances in science and technology. He is no unstudied proponent of growth and progress for their sake alone, but rather a man who recognizes the dual potential for benefit and harm in virtually all modern technologies. Implicit in all of Sakharov's reform proposals is the theme that rational thought must govern progress if the beneficial potential of science and technology is not to be lost in the mad scramble for growth and industrial giantism.

The real problem with the Slavophile-Westernizer frame of reference lies less with the "fit" of the respective authors into the appropriate categories than with the direction in which this particular turn of mind leads the analysis. Even Western students of Russian and Soviet history are sometimes tempted to regard that vast nation as a thing apart, following its own inherent and unique pattern of historical evolution. To frame the Solzhenitsyn-Sakharov dialogue in Slavophile and Westernizer terms is to succumb to that temptation; while the historical analogy is fascinating and tells us something about the durability of certain frames of reference, it also leads us away from the even more intriguing and intellectually fruitful comparison of the elements of the Solzhenitsyn-Sakharov dialogue with a prolonged discussion in the West about the nature and future of contemporary industrial society. Although it is certainly beyond the scope of this conclusion to encompass all that has been said in that discussion—many of the themes have reappeared in differing incarnations since the beginning of industrialization itself—it is possible to identify certain recurring strains of the argument and to discuss the ways in which they are reflected in the writings of Solzhenitsyn and Sakharov.

SCIENCE, TECHNOLOGY, AND PROGRESS

It is in the realm of science, technology, and progress that the writings of Solzhenitsyn and Sakharov most visibly reflect an ongoing discussion about the fate of industrial society elsewhere in the world. Perhaps because the topics which arise deal with palpable issues that confront virtually all modern societies, and perhaps because these questions touch upon the most immediately visible impact of science and technology on our everyday lives, the links between the Solzhenitsyn-Sakharov dialogue and parallel discussions in other industrial nations are readily apparent. Significantly, an increasingly lively debate has emerged within the last decade among officially sanctioned Soviet scholars themselves, and while they eventually reach predictably optimistic conclusions that science and technology are positive and manageable forces, they, too, raise, if only in passing, many of the questions that occupy the dissidents and their Western counterparts.[5]

The most pervasive of these issues is the impact of science and technology on society *writ large*, whether conceptualized in terms of the subtle impact on culture and the sociopolitical order or the more obvious and direct impact on the economy and environment. Both Solzhenitsyn and Sakharov share reservations also commonly expressed in the West about the deleterious impact of contemporary technology, although they are at opposite poles on the intensely debated question of an appropriate response. In the Western literature, one finds three recurring themes which are also expressed by both dissident authors: (1) an examination of the social and environmental costs of uncontrolled technologies,[6] (2) a fear that what Langdon Winner has termed "autonomous technology" may assume a dynamic of its own beyond the control of either rational planners or existing traditional cultures,[7] and (3) a willingness, indeed, a demand, that the conventional growth model be scrapped or revised.[8] In the first instance, the visible impact of industrial technology and its voracious appetite for resources have been lamented by a long list of Western commentators, including Barry Commoner, who first noted the increasingly hazardous presence of new industrial technologies after World War II; Paul Ehrlich, who saw portending doom in the synergistic interaction of population, affluence, and technology; and the Club of Rome, which has issued dire projections concerning the adaptability of industrial society.[9] Yet, on the other side of the issue, Western commentators such as Herman Kahn offer more optimistic projections, arguing that mankind can adapt to new social imperatives and that new technologies and resource substitution can always be counted upon to ameliorate the impact of previous technologies and compensate for the dwindling store of conventional resources.[10]

The fear of "autonomous technology" also haunts both the

dissident and Western discussions, whether in the form of a blatant technology-centered economic and social order in which the imperatives of technology shape overtly or covertly all other social and economic relationships, or in the more subtle form of the pursuit of technological modernization for its own sake. While the implicit discussion of this theme is less visible in the writings of Solzhenitsyn and Sakharov than in some of the Western literature, it is clearly present, as expressed in the former's concern about the pervasive "scientization" of society and in the latter's lament that the development of science and technology in the Soviet Union is in the hands of narrow-minded officials who do not ponder the larger implications of their actions. At the very least, however, each author expresses the notion that technological imperatives, whether intellectualized as the conventional wisdom of the day or operative *sub rosa* because of the scientization of the culture itself, have acquired a self-sustaining and potentially deleterious dynamic of their own.[11]

The conventional growth model, and the very notion of progress, upon which it is premised, are also open to critical examination in both the dissident and Western dialogues. At one extreme, the proponents of zero growth reject the conventional model and argue instead for the creation of a "steady state" system in which careful controls over technology and the recycling of resources will maintain equilibrium.[12] In such a setting, further modernization is still possible through technological advances to higher levels of sophistication, provided that appropriate safeguards maintain equilibrium at any point in time. To differing degrees, both Solzhenitsyn and Sakharov reflect elements of this view in their own projections for the future, although their notions of what constitute appropriate safeguards are at odds. For Solzhenitsyn, the shift to the Northeast and the creation of manageable, environmentally integrated communities provide for the selective utilization of advanced technologies, although it is obvious that the author's principal focus is on the psychological and morale building aspects of these new settlements, rather than on their technological sophistication. Appropriate controls will presumably emerge from the community itself, an argument similar to what James D. Carroll has labeled "participatory technology" and Ivan Illich has termed a "convivial society." For his part, Sakharov rejects the more extreme zero-growth model as both inappropriate and impossible to attain, opting instead for a rational comprehension of the concept of progress, with guidance provided not by community per se but by the scientific elite. His position is therefore similar to that of the technology assessment and futures movement, which emphasizes a diverse assortment of sophisticated models and procedures designed to plot technological and socioeconomic trends.[13]

SOCIETY, POLITICS, AND CULTURE

Many themes concerning society, politics, and culture which are at the center of attention in the Solzhenitsyn-Sakharov dialogue also find direct reflection in the Western discussion of the nature of the contemporary industrial order. At the root of much of this commentary on both sides is what Maurice Stein has termed "the eclipse of community," that is, the notion that community has been lost both as a viable expression of social organization and as a psychological touchstone for the definition of self in the modern world.[14] As in the Solzhenitsyn-Sakharov dialogue, Western commentators respond to this loss either by describing appropriate "higher" or more mature forms of community, most often premised on the ultilization of advanced technology and a high level of social planning, or by recommending the resuscitation of the "old" sense of community, often at the deliberate expense of other economic or social goals. The range of the discussion in the West is virtually too broad to encompass within a brief conclusion; while some reformers stress the revitalization of the psychological sense of community, others focus more upon its economic and social determinants.[15] At the least, all such reformulations entail both a serious challenge to the economic order —although whether that order is redefined for sociopolitical or ecological ends is frequently a matter of dispute—and to the definition of the place of the individual within the social milieu.

The latter issue also raises the question of the redefinition of the private and public spheres of life. However quietly and subtly, every major redefinition of the social and cultural order has also had direct bearing on the boundary between the private and public aspects of one's activities, and implicit in much of the Western

discussion of the fate of modern society are the seemingly paradoxical themes of the increasing privatization of life on the one
hand—a privatization that is as often condemned for its narcissism
as applauded for its proliferation of opportunities and lifestyles—
and the growing incursion of public concerns into what were
traditionally viewed as private spheres. In the West, the issue is
most clearly seen in the tension between the opportunities created
by affluence to devote increasing time to purely private concerns,
and the ever more taut economic and sociopolitical network in
which heretofore private actions affect public goals. For Solzhenitsyn and Sakharov the tension between the public and private
selves is understandably linked more to one's involvement in
dissident activities than to the more subtle issues of mutual self-
control and regulation. Yet Solzhenitsyn's attention to the wholly
private internal struggles through which the new "spiritual elite"
is born and his concept of self-limitation, all cast within the larger
framework of a sense of responsibility to society, clearly reflect
an awareness of the symbiotic relationship between the private
and public selves, as does Sakharov's assertion that one must
assume personal responsibility for the consequences of acting
out one's public role.[16]

The failure of reform efforts in modern industrial societies is
also a common theme which links the Solzhenitsyn-Sakharov
dialogue to its counterparts in the West.[17] Whether envisioned
historically as the attempt to modify the institutions of nascent
industrial states along humanistic and democratic lines, leading to
the emergence of what may be broadly termed the liberal democracies of the West, or as more fundamental attempts to re-
structure socioeconomic institutions and, through them, to alter
the basic nature of mankind, leading eventually to the emergence
of communist or other millenarian societies, such reforms were
once thought to embody the only hope for dealing with the myriad
problems facing the newly industrialized nations at the beginning
of the current century. But as the century progressed, the mood of
hope and optimism that had greeted reformers of either disposition
perceptibly soured. The international order collapsed, leading to
world war; the industrial might of the most advanced nations was
not sufficient to prevent depression and social discord; and poli-

tically, the older democracies were put to the most severe test of their history, while most of the newer ones fell to extremist movements from the right. On the political left, a similar process of disillusion was at work. The Socialist Internationale quickly gave way to a series of coups and rebellions, with only the Russian experiment surviving in highly distorted form through the emergence of the Leninist vanguard party and the even more strident formulations of the Stalin years.

If the first wave of disillusion were seen principally as a political failure—that is, that the processes and institutions in which such hopes had been invested had yielded unpredictable and largely undesirable results—then the second wave came more in the recognition of the intellectual failure of modern man to comprehend and manipulate his world. Whether on the right or left in political terms, hopeful reformers came from the 1920s onward to look upon the emergence of what may be termed "social technologies" of economics, planning, and sociology as providing the tools by which a rational society could manage its affairs. In part because such tools were presented as apolitical in nature—in fact, "above" politics, as most of their earlier proponents would argue—and in part because they stressed man's presumably growing command of the economic and social environment, they came to be regarded as the keys to further social reform. While they seemingly enjoyed considerable success when first applied—boom and bust business cycles were brought under control and meaningful social programs were undertaken—and even if the "new deals" or "great societies" they heralded never completely fulfilled expectations, it was hard not to accept the conclusion that a productive beginning had been made through the application of such social technologies. By the 1970s, however, the luster had worn off these social technologies, in part because they no longer seemed to provide easy answers for vexing economic and social problems, and in part because, in the hands of the self-proclaimed "best and brightest" that had applied them, they brought disturbing new problems and commitments.[18]

To varying degrees, Solzhenitsyn and Sakharov also evidence important elements of these themes. Most obviously, the former rejects the entire notion of humanistic and political reforms as both doomed to failure and wrongly aimed at social, economic, or political problems rather than the spiritual rebirth of a coherent nation. Perhaps understandably, his reading of Russian history suggests that in such a setting reformers quickly become militant revolutionaries, and such revolutionaries become a new generation of autocrats. Sakharov's position is much more complex, befitting the inherent tension in his hope that man's rational faculties can plan a better social and political order and his conclusion that the essentially sound notions of socialism have been perverted by the present leadership. In part, the tension is resolved by investing the principal leading roles in Sakharov's ideal society into the hands of the scientific and technocratic elites, which presumably are most capable of developing rational decisions and least susceptible to the "frenzy" of politics.

Another fundamental issue which has appeared repeatedly in the Western discussion is the nature and distribution of political power in an advanced industrial state. Two trends have been evident in dealing with these issues. On the one hand, some theorists have attempted to redefine both the scope of legitimacy of and the mechanisms for mass involvement in the political process. Whether done in the activist vein of what came in the 1960s to be called "participatory democracy," more subtly accomplished through concepts such as entitlement or social equity, or merely tacitly assumed as a consequence of the increasing politicization of the society as a whole, this new mass involvement both alters the nature of the political community and provides the justification for a substantial devolution of real power downward through the sociopolitical hierarchy. Not surprisingly, very little of this thinking is reflected in the writings of either Solzhenitsyn or Sakharov; the most elusive figures in the political discourse of each are indeed the common man or woman who will constitute the mass of a new social order. For Solzhenitsyn, this element is seen principally as the passive custodian of a sense of Russian nationalism, while for Sakharov, it emerges as a potentially democratic force initially requiring the careful leadership of the scientific elite. But little else is said of its long-term role in political life.

The second development in Western thought is far more faithfully reflected in the Solzhenitsyn-Sakharov dialogue. It is the attempt to fashion both a new definition of elite legitimacy and to explain the emergence of new elites to replace those of the older social order. The most prominent example in Western theory is the emergence of the notion of the technocrat-manager as the consummate political figure in modern society. While hardly a new phenomenon in itself—Saint-Simon raised a very similar sort of argument—the development of the concept of a "technocracy" and the enhanced role of the technocratic elite are given added force both by the failure of "political" reforms per se and the demonstrably greater complexity of the problems which must be solved by a modern industrial society. In such a setting, scientists, technicians, and managers increasingly come to influence the making of public policy because of the relevance of their skills, with their ultimate role seen either in terms of their rise to political power itself or in terms of their indispensable behind-the-scenes role. It is equally significant that the implications of the technocratic model have also engendered a counter model emphasizing the revitalization of traditional elites.[19]

Perhaps more clearly than any of the other elements of the Western discussion, the traditional elite versus the technocrat conflict is seen in the Solzhenitsyn-Sakharov dialogue. Indeed, it is this critical question, of who will be the carriers of social and political values and who will ultimately inherit a legitimate right to govern, that is at the root of their differing views of political life. Their common devotion to the notions of human rights and the free competition of ideas does little to mollify their irreconcilable differences on this issue; just as virtually all of the Western discussions have finally resolved themselves into the critical questions of who rules, and with what right, so too does the Solzhenitsyn-Sakharov dialogue arrive at the same point. What is striking, at least in the overview, is the similarity between the two discussions.

NOTES

1. Although there are many histories of the two movements, the best overview is Franco Venturi, *Roots of Revolution* (New York: Knopf, 1960).

2. Stephen Carter, *The Politics of Solzhenitsyn* (New York: Holmes and Meier, 1977), pp. 141–44.

3. Ibid.

4. Ibid.

5. *See* works such as *Nauchno-tekhnicheskaia revoliutsiia i sotsial'nyi progress* (Moscow: Nauka, 1977); A. Artobolevskii, et al., *Partiia i sovremenniia nauchno-teknicheskaia revoliutsiia v SSSR* (Moscow, Politizdat, 1974), *Chelovek-nauka-tekhnika* (Moscow: Politizdat, 1973): and *The Scientific and Technological Revolution: Social Effects and Prospects* (Moscow: Progress, 1972). The best English-language survey is Julian M. Cooper, "The Scientific and Technological Revolution in Soviet Theory," in *Technology and Communist Culture: The Socio-Cultural Impact of Technology under Socialism*, ed. Frederic J. Fleron (New York: Praeger, 1977), pp. 146–80.

6. Ginzberg, ed., *Technology and Social Change* (New York: Columbia University Press, 1963); S. Hetzler, *Technological Growth and Social Change* (New York: Praeger, 1969); E. J. Mishan, *Technology and Growth: The Price We Pay* (London: Praeger, 1970); Jacques Ellul, *The Technological Society* (New York: Vintage, 1964); Bernard Gendron, *Technology and the Human Condition* (New York: St. Martins, 1977); Ina Spiegel-Rosing and Derek de Solla Price, *Science, Technology, and Society: A Cross-Disciplinary Perspective* (Beverly Hills: Sage, 1977); and Philip L. Bereano, ed., *Technology as a Social and Political Phenomenon* (New York: Wiley, 1976).

7. Langdon Winner, *Autonomous Technology: Technics-Out-of-Control as a Theme in Political Thought* (Cambridge, Mass.: MIT Press, 1977).

8. Robert Nisbet, *History of the Idea of Progress* (New York: Basic Books, 1980); *see also* the two-volume discussion edited by Willem L. Oltmans, *On Growth: One* and *On Growth: Two* (New York: Capricorn, 1975).

9. Barry Commoner, *The Closing Circle: Nature, Man and Technology* (New York: Knopf, 1971); Paul R. Ehrlich and Anne H. Ehrlich, *Population, Resources, Environment: Issues in Human Ecology* (San Francisco: W. H. Freeman, 1972); D. H. Meadows et al., *The Limits to Growth* (New York: Universe, 1972); H. S. D. Cole et al., *Models of Doom: A Critique of the Limits to Growth* (New York: Universe, 1973). For the orthodox Soviet response to the latter, which suprisingly includes some proenvironmental and antigrowth sentiments, *see* Donald R. Kelley, "Economic Growth and Environmental Quality: The Soviet Reaction to *The Limits to Growth*," *Canadian Slavonic Papers* 28, no. 3 (1976), pp. 266–83.

10. Herman Kahn, et al., *The Next 200 Years: A Scenario for America*

and the World (New York: Morrow, 1976); Herman Kahn and Anthony J. Wiener, *The Year 2000* (New York: Macmillan, 1967).

11. Winner, *Autonomous Technology*; Gendron, *Technology and the Human Condition*, pp. 148-62.

12. William Ophuls, *Ecology and the Politics of Scarcity* (San Francisco: W. H. Freeman, 1977); Herman E. Daly, *Steady-State Economics* (San Francisco: W. H. Freeman, 1977); Edward F. Renshaw, *The End of Progress: Adjusting to a No-Growth Economy* (North Scituate, Mass.: Duxbury, 1976); and Dennis C. Pirages and Paul R. Ehrlich, *Ark II: Social Response to Environmental Imperatives* (San Francisco: W. H. Freeman, 1974).

13. James D. Carroll, "Participatory Technology," *Science* 171 (February 19, 1971), pp. 647-53; Ivan Illich, *Tools for Conviviality* (New York: Harper and Row, 1973); Edward Cornish, *The Study of the Future* (Washtion: World Future Society, 1977); Alvin Toffler, *The Futurists* (New York; Random House, 1972); and R. W. Prehoda, *Designing the Future: The Role of Technological Forecasting* (Philadelphia: Chilton, 1967).

14. Maurice R. Stein, *The Eclipse of Community: An Interpretation of American Studies* (Princeton, N.J.: Princeton University Press, 1960).

15. See, for example, Theodore Roszak, *The Making of a Counter Culture: Reflections on a Technocratic Society and Its Youthful Opposition* (New York: Doubleday, 1969); Charles A. Reich, *The Greening of America* (New York: Random House, 1970); and Alvin Toffler, *The Third Wave* (New York: Morrow, 1980).

16. Alvin Toffler, *Future Shock* (New York: Random House, 1970), esp. chaps. 6 and 17; Peter Berger, Briditte Berger, and Hansfried Kellner, *The Homeless Mind: Modernization and Consciousness* (New York: Random House, 1974); Theodore Lowi, *Private Life and Public Order* (New York: Norton, 1968).

17. Reich, *Greening of America*, pp. 41-58; Zbigniew Brzezinski, *Between Two Ages: America's Role in the Technetronic Era* (New York: Penguin, 1970), pp. 195-254; Theodore Lowi, *The End of Liberalism* (New York: Norton, 1969).

18. Robert Boguslaw, *The New Utopians: A Study of System Design and Social Change* (Englewood Cliffs, N.J.: Prentice-Hall, 1965); Otis L. Graham, Jr., *Toward a Planned Society: From Roosevelt to Nixon* (New York: Oxford University Press, 1976); Ida R. Hoos, *Systems Analysis in Public Policy* (Berkeley: University of California Press, 1972); Jeffrey D. Straussman, *The Limits of Technocratic Politics* (New Brunswick, N.J.: Transaction, 1978); and Marvin E. Gettleman and David Mermelstein, eds., *The Great Society Reader: The Failure of American Liberalism* (New York: Random House, 1967).

19. Jean Meynaud, *Technocracy* (New York: Free Press, 1969); Ellul, *Technological Society*, pp. 248–84; Bereano, *Social and Political Phenomenon*, pp. 440–538; Godfrey Boyle, David Elliott, and Robin Roy, eds., *The Politics of Technology* (New York: Longman, 1977); Straussman, *Limits of Technocratic Politics*; Daniel Bell, *The Coming of Post Industrial Society* (New York: Basic Books, 1973), pp. 339–68; and Leon N. Lindberg, *Politics and the Future of Industrial Society* (New York: David McKay, 1976).

Bibliographic Essay

The publication of Solzhenitsyn's literary and historical works has proven to be a controversial endeavor. Even setting aside the controversy that surrounded those few works published by *Novy Mir* in the Soviet Union itself, disputes have continuously arisen over the accuracy of texts sent abroad before 1974, publication rights in the West, and the quality of the translations themselves. The most complete bibliographic essays to date are those by Alexis Klimoff and John B. Dunlop, which appear in John B. Dunlop et al., eds., *Alexandr Solzhenitsyn: Critical Essays and Documentary Materials,* second edition, first published by Nordland Press in 1973 and then reissued in enlarged form by Collier Books in the United States and Collier Macmillan in Great Britain, both in 1975. Dunlop and his collaborators are now at work on a companion volume dealing with Solzhenitsyn's writings since his exile in 1974, forthcoming by Nordland Press.

The most complete Russian-language collection of Solzhenitsyn's works available at present is *Sobranie sochinenii* [*Collected Works*], six volumes, published in Frankfurt by Posev Verlag in 1969–1970. Solzhenitsyn has always objected to this "pirated" and now obviously out-of-date edition and is assembling a nine-volume collection to be published in 1981 or 1982 by YMCA Press in Paris, his favorite publisher for Russian-language texts in the West.

Competing Russian-language editions of *Cancer Ward* and *The First Circle* appeared in the West, convincing Solzhenitsyn that it was dangerous to trust the fate of his manuscripts to others abroad. In the former case, numerous copies of the *samizdat* version made their way to the West, making it impossible for the author to control publication rights or the quality of translations. Two unauthorized Russian-language editions appeared, one published by the YMCA Press in 1968 and the other by Posev Verlag in the same year. Multiple Russian editions were also offered of *The First Circle*, which Solzhenitsyn had tried in vain to control more completely than *Cancer Ward*. YMCA Press and Posev Verlag again produced competing volumes, issued in 1969, and a third was offered by the London-based Flegon Press in the same year.

YMCA Press has played the leading role in publishing the author's works ever since Solzhenitsyn secured the services of a literary representative to maintain control over publication rights. YMCA editions have included: *Pismo vozhdiam Sovetskogo Soiuza* [Letter to the Soviet leaders], 1974; *Lenin v. Tsiurikhe* [Lenin in Zurich], 1975; *Iz pod glub* [From under the rubble), 1974; *Bodalsia telenok s dubom* [The oak and the calf], 1975; *Arkipelag Gulag, I–VII* [The gulag archipelago, I–VII], 1973, 1974, and 1976; and *Avgust chetyrnadtsatogo* [August 1914], 1971.

The translation of Solzhenitsyn's early works into English was a haphazard phenomenon, with competing publishers rushing to complete frequently questionable translations in order to capture the curious American and British markets. No fewer than five versions of *One Day in the Life of Ivan Denisovich* are available: the translation by Max Hayward and Donald Hingley, published in New York by Praeger in 1963 and issued in paperback by Bantam in 1969; Ralph Parker's translation, published in New York by Dutton and in London by Gollancz, both in 1963, and issued in paperback by Signet in 1971; the translation by Thomas P. Whitney, released in New York by Fawcett in 1963, with simultaneous paperback by Crest; Bela von Block's translation, published in New York by Lancer in 1963 and by Lodestone in 1973; and the translation by Gillon Aitken, issued by Farrar, Straus and Giroux in New York in 1971.

The most complete collection of Solzhenitsyn's short stories and "prose poems," including "Matryona's House," "For the Good of the Cause," and "An Incident at Krechetovka Station," is provided in Michael Glenny's *Alexander Solzhenitsyn: Stories and Prose Poems*, New York: Farrar, Straus, and Giroux, 1971; issued in paperback by Bantam the following year. The only similar volume is *"We Never Make Mistakes": Two Short Novels*, translated by Paul W. Blackstock and published by the University of North Carolina Press in 1973, with the paperback by Norton in 1971.

Two translations of *Cancer Ward* appeared in the West. The British publisher Bodley Head brought out a two-volume effort, released in 1968 and 1969, translated by Nicholas Bethell and David Burg; this edition was subsequently published as a single volume in the United States by Farrar, Straus and Giroux in 1969 and released as a Bantam paperback the same year. The second version came from an unknown translator working under the pseudonym "Rebecca Frank" and was published in New York by Dial Press in 1968, with a paperback edition by Dell in 1973.

The First Circle similarly appeared in two competing English translations. The first to appear, in 1968, was offered by an anonymous translator calling himself "Michael Guybon," whose efforts were published in London by Collins; a paperback was subsequently published by Fontana in 1970. The American edition was translated by Thomas P. Whitney and issued by Harper and Row in 1968, with a paperback from Bantam the following year.

Solzhenitsyn's *Gulag Archipelago* was published in a three-volume set in Great Britain by Harvill beginning in 1974, with paperback editions by Fontana first appearing two years later. Harper and Row published the American edition in both hard-cover and paperback beginning in 1974. Both the British and American translations are by Thomas P. Whitney.

Solzhenitsyn's *Letter to the Soviet Leaders* was published in Britain by the Index on Censorship, with American rights granted to Harper and Row. Both editions appeared in 1974 and were translated by Hilary Sternberg.

Solzhenitsyn's more expressly political tracts have been published by a number of houses. The British edition of *From Under the Rubble* was brought out by Harvill in 1975, and the American

version was published by Little, Brown the same year. Both translations were the work of a team headed by A. M. Brock, working
under the direction of Michael Scammell. *Warning to the West,*
which contained speeches to American and British audiences in
1975 and 1976, was published by Bodley Head in London
and Farrar, Straus and Giroux in New York, both in 1976; the
translators were Harris L. Coulter and Nataly Martin. *A World
Split Apart: Commencement Address Delivered at Harvard
University, June 8, 1978* was published in a joint Russian and
English version by Harper and Row in the same year, translated
by Irina Ilovayaskaya Alberti, with the assistance of Alexis Klimoff.
The author's most recent political commentary has appeared in
his article "Misconceptions About Russia Are a Threat to America,"
which appeared in *Foreign Affairs* 58, number 4 (Spring, 1980),
and was published in book form by Harper and Row, with a
"slightly revised translation," under the title *The Mortal Danger;*
the translators were Michael Nicholson and Alexis Klimoff.

*The Oak and the Calf: Sketches on Literary Life in the Soviet
Union,* which is Solzhenitsyn's most direct venture into autobiography, was published by Collins and Harvill in London and
Harper and Row in New York, both editions appearing in 1980
and translated by Harry Willetts.

Andrei Sakharov's writings have avoided the controversy that
surrounded the publication and translation of Solzhenitsyn's
works. Original Russian-language sources are most easily available through the *Arkhiv samizdata,* a continuing publication and
indexing service prepared by the Research Department of Radio
Liberty, although unfortunately there is no single-volume collection
of his essays in Russian. Only his 1968 essay *Progress, Coexistence,
and Intellectual Freedom* has been issued in Russian in book form
by Posev Verlag in Frankfurt. The best bibliographical essay on
Sakharov's writings, including his earlier scientific works, appears
in Peter Dornan's "Andrei Sakharov: The Conscience of a Liberal
Scientist," in Rudolf L. Tokes, ed., *Dissent in the USSR: Politics,
Ideology, and People,* published in 1975 by Johns Hopkins University Press.

Sakharov's *Progress, Coexistence, and Intellectual Freedom* was first published in the United States by Norton in 1968, with an introduction, afterword, and notes by Harrison E. Salisbury. The British edition, offered by Pelican, appeared the following year. The remainder of his writings are most easily accessible in English through edited volumes. The first, which reproduces the 1968 essay and contains memoranda, public statements, and interviews from 1970 to 1974, appears under the title *Sakharov Speaks*, edited by Harrison E. Salisbury and published in the United States by Knopf in hard cover and by Vintage in paperback in 1974. The British edition was issued by Harvill in the same year.

Sakharov's next major contribution came in the form of a somewhat rambling essay entitled *My Country and the World*, in which he reviewed both internal developments in the USSR and related world events. The translation was prepared by Guy V. Daniels, and Knopf published the hardcover edition in the United States, with Vintage once again offering the paperback, both in 1975. In Britain, Harvill also released the book in 1975.

The most recently published collection of Sakharov's writings and public statements through the summer of 1977 is *Alarm and Hope*, edited by Efrem Yankelevich and Alfred Friendly, Jr., and published in the United States by Vintage in 1978. This work contains both Sakharov's 1975 Nobel Prize lecture and a series of comments on the increasing suppression of dissidents in the USSR. The author's briefly optimistic correspondence with President Carter is also discussed at length. Collins published the British edition in 1979.

Index

About the Author

Donald R. Kelley, Associate Professor and Chairman of the Department of Political Science at the University of Arkansas in Fayetteville, has written extensively on Soviet life and politics. He is the author of *The Economic Superpowers and the Environment* and the editor of and contributor to two anthologies on Soviet life and the environment. Kelley has published articles in the *Journal of Politics*, the *American Political Science Review*, and several anthologies.